THE PREPPER'S
GUIDE TO RIFLES

THE PREPPER'S GUIDE TO RIFLES

HOW TO PROPERLY CHOOSE, MAINTAIN, AND USE THESE FIREARMS IN EMERGENCY SITUATIONS

ROBERT K. CAMPBELL

Skyhorse Publishing

Skyhorse Publishing books may be purchased in bulk at special discounts for sales promotion, corporate gifts, fund-raising, or educational purposes. Special editions can also be created to specifications. For details, contact the Special Sales Department, Skyhorse Publishing, 307 West 36th Street, 11th Floor, New York, NY 10018 or info@ skyhorsepublishing.com.

Skyhorse® and Skyhorse Publishing® are registered trademarks of Skyhorse Publishing, Inc.®, a Delaware corporation.

Visit our website at www.skyhorsepublishing.com.

10 9 8 7 6 5 4 3 2 1

Library of Congress Cataloging-in-Publication Data is available on file.

Cover design by Tom Lau
Cover photos courtesy of Sako, Weatherby, and Wilson Combat

Print ISBN: 978-1-5107-1398-7
Ebook ISBN: 978-1-5107-1402-1

Printed in China

CONTENTS

DEDICATION

It is to the hills I look and from there comes my help. Thank God I am able to do the work I love and love the work.

Thanks to my wonderful children for their help and, for the first time, thanks to the grandchildren for helping with the shooting and making the book a reality.

And always to a gentle and loving spirit, Joyce.

—Robert Campbell

INTRODUCTION

As I began this book I realized that the reporter must gather information beneficial to himself first. I looked to my early reading on firearms, hunting, and personal defense. Little was written concerning the rifle for personal defense. The rifle is the best means we have of defending the home, the farm, and the country. The handgun, although useful, is difficult to master, and the shotgun is at its best at close range. Recoil is a problem with both, but not so much with a properly chosen rifle. This work covers hunting and competition to a degree, but it is primarily concerned with personal defense. The subject takes a lifetime to study and master, but I think you will understand the subject better after you read this book.

Meaningful performance, both human and mechanical, is analyzable, and thus the book is divided into two parts. The human part of the book focuses on marksmanship. Marksmanship is important, even vital, but gun handling is more important at combat ranges. Quickly getting into action and properly handling the rifle is everything inside of 50 yards. Marksmanship is more important in hunting and competition. Quick, efficient gun handling saves lives.

I hope this information is easily comprehensible. The technical descriptions of mechanical actions, firearms, and ammunition performance are as free as possible from the kind of technical jargon that renders text incoherent. While those "in the know" enjoy using these terms, common language allows seamless movement through the text. In this book, speculation isn't given the same footing as facts and knowledge. Range testing is done with accuracy, and reliability is stressed. The testing is both repeatable and verifiable by qualified shooters. For many years, I have learned to accept criticism, and use it to sharpen my views. So I have been as explicit as possible in certain accounts and explanations. When it comes to understanding conceptual complexities, there is room for interpretation concerning training and movement. Optics firearms and ammunition may be tested using the scientific method. The adoption of science in reporting makes for flawless application.

I do not like to point out the allegedly correct choice in gear, but instead give the reader the means to make his own best choice. Rifles may be chosen based on individual tastes so long as the rifle is reliable and accurate. All such good choices could not be covered in this book, but none of the poor choices are found in these pages. I hope to give the reader a system for grounding knowledge based on experience and empirical data to choose the right rifle and accessories. It is always fair for the reader to ask how knowledge is acquired. The answer is that extensive reading and scholarship in the subject is coupled with field experience—in this case, forty years of study and experience. Yet from those thousands of articles and a dozen books, little has been simply repeated in these pages. This is fresh research, and while I respect classic rifles and enjoy them, for the most part I have used the newest gear. Moreover, since this work is focused on *personal defense* and *beginning shooters*, the way to the right path doesn't include a lot of influence from Cooper, Keith, or O'Connor. It is quite all right to begin on your own, and to make your own decisions.

To master the rifle takes discipline. A marksman with a second-rate rifle in a minor caliber is more formidable than a duffer with a great rifle. Some spend a great deal of money on expensive gear only to have it in large part wasted by not putting forth the necessary effort in learning the rifle. We end up with the same old play and a new cast of comedians. A good rifle on the shoulder is a great comfort, but more so if you know how to use it.

There is much motivation to learn the rifle simply from reading current headlines. Takeover robbers, home invaders, spree killers, gangs, and terrorists tend to be heavily armed. We need to be prepared. Much of my work applies to peace officers. Such officers in small- to medium-sized jurisdictions are most often on their own in training. They will usually purchase their own rifles, and they aren't insignificant investments. Bean counters do not like training time and find it cheaper to bury cops than train them. The best marksmen in the Thin Blue Line are self-taught. The majority supply their own firearms and need to make informed choices. While I will always retain a proud connection with the Thin Blue Line, this book is informative to every reader. A real need may exist to be armed—including for the purpose of exercising your rights—and the challenge of mastering the rifle is always a good motivation for achieving another rung on the ladder of self-defense.

CHAPTER ONE

SAFETY

Firearm safety is the single set of rules and actions that must be mastered before we attempt to achieve proficiency at arms. Firearm safety is the equivalent of looking before you back up the truck, or making certain the hand is out of the way of the chainsaw blade. Some approach firearms with uncertainty and apprehension. There is

This rifle has the bolt locked to the rear and the magazine is removed. It is still treated as if it were loaded.

no more reason to do so than to fear learning to drive a manual shift truck or a Honda Civic. This fear is self-induced and must be replaced with competence with the firearm. A healthy respect for any machine is part of safe handling.

Practice will eliminate accidental discharges. There are no such incidents as accidental discharges; the correct term is negligent discharge, and the unplanned firing of the weapon is a result of negligence in handling. Practice with the correct safety procedure eliminates negligent handling. Everyone admires great competence, but I have also seen gun handling that sent a chill down my spine and made me openly question the shooter's intelligence. There is a tendency of human beings to resent rigid conventions. In music and politics this is admirable—but not in gun handling. If you follow the safety rules, a firearm may sometimes fire when unintended, but the occasional stuck firing pin or high cartridge primer occurs so infrequently that this will not be as great a hazard when the shooter has practiced strict muzzle discipline. For those who do not adhere to the rules, well, I like to have a couple of zip codes between them and me, and I am not shy about ejecting them from the range. I have had students who have raised my blood pressure to previously unheard of levels. Needless to say, they did not pass the course.

PRIMARY SAFETY RULES

There are as many as a dozen safety rules posted at firing ranges. Many dictate safe entry and egress and the types of firearms that may be used. Some ranges limit speed shooting or rapid fire. There are many considerations, but the four I enumerate are the basics from which all others flow.

All Guns Are Always Loaded

When handling the firearm, the trigger finger is off the trigger until you fire.

Even if the firearm has been triple checked, always treat the firearm as if it were loaded and capable of firing with a pull of the trigger. Always execute proper trigger discipline, *keeping the finger off the trigger until you are actually going to fire.* By always adhering to these rules, you need not adopt a second set of rules with loaded firearms. The same rules apply to stored, unloaded, or training rifles as the rules observed on a hot range, where the guns are loaded and in use. When checking a rifle, the NRA way is used: The action is open and the forefinger reaches into the chamber to be certain that the chamber isn't loaded. The magazine well is checked for a magazine or cartridges.

The finger is off the trigger and the bolt locked back before we load the Ruger 10/22.

This shooter is learning to check both the magazine well and chamber to determine if the rifle is loaded.

The beginner must learn the manual of arms of each rifle and how to properly lock the bolt to the rear—if it will lock. Some designs will not.

There is one acceptable chamber check with the finger.

Keep the Finger off the Trigger Until you Fire

The trigger finger never touches the trigger until you fire. Not when you *think* you will fire or when you are *going* to fire but **only when you fire**. This rule will keep things safe; when you are hunting or engaged in a personal defense situation, this rule is particularly important. Walking around with the trigger finger in register is the mark of an incompetent.

These operators are training with their fingers off the trigger. (Colt Defense)

Never Point a Firearm at Anything you do not Wish to Shoot

This is called muzzle discipline. The muzzle must not cover anything you will not shoot, and it must not cover any part of your body. The muzzle should be pointed toward the ground, with the action broken open and the chamber empty when approaching the firing line,

This shooter has his eye on the target and his finger off the trigger.

when the rifle is stored in the home, or when the rifle is being carried. The rule is constant when the rifle is loaded and ready for action. When used operationally, such as in the hunting field or for personal defense, this rule is particularly important.

Know Your Backstop

This rule applies to all firearms. The rifle is much more powerful than a handgun or shotgun; it will penetrate structures and other items that the pistol bullet or shotgun slug will not, particularly at long range. The training range should have a tall backstop. If you use steel targets, make certain that the target will stop a rifle bullet. Those aspiring to a complicated trade must learn the basics, and recognizing the properties of the rifle

This 100-yard range features a formidable berm.

and the backstop is important. Never fire at the flat earth or at water. A rifle bullet may ricochet with plenty of energy left to remain lethal.

The Rifle is on "Safe" Until You Fire

Do not trust a manual safety alone! After all, it is made by man and may malfunction. Just the same, the manual safety is a good hedge against accidental discharge, but does not take the place of trigger discipline. This is particularly important for those hunting with the rifle and engaged in three-gun competition and tactical movement.

OTHER SAFETY RULES

Use the Correct Ammunition

Understand the difference between the .223 and 5.56mm chambers, as well as the .308 and 7.62 × 51mm NATO. Do not use heavy loads in old firearms. Be certain the caliber is proper for the gun. It is quite possible to accidentally fire similar rifle cartridges in the wrong chamber, and the result is often catastrophic. I cannot enumerate each combination—that would take another

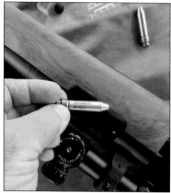

When in doubt or when building a rifle, always use a chamber gauge.

Brownells offers first class chamber gauges that answer many safety questions.

volume—but be certain of your rifle and its proper chambering. As just one example, recently I examined a World War II Mauser Karabiner 98k. The stock was marked 7.62. Most who examined the rifle would have thought it was one of the Israeli rifles re-barreled to 7.62 NATO, as it had all the characteristics and markings. But a headspace gauge showed that the rifle was chambered for the 8mm Mauser (also known as 7.92×57mm Mauser). Mismatched stocks are not uncommon. The older the rifle the more we must research.

Be Cautious of Hang Fires

If the firing pin strikes the cartridge but the cartridge fails to fire, wait a solid minute before racking the bolt and clearing the chamber. I have experienced a dozen or so hang fires over the years, primarily with surplus ammunition. The primer is struck, but somehow the powder does not immediately ignite. A second later—*BANG!* You can imagine what would happen if you opened the breech and the cartridge ignited.

Always Wear Eye and Ear Protection When Firing

Shards of brass, bullets, and even hot and hardened lubricants are thrown toward the shooter by the reciprocating action. Always wear good hearing protection to protect precious senses, and quality eye glasses to save your eyesight.

Proper hearing and eye protection must be worn at all times when using any firearm.

Check for Barrel Obstructions

Rifles are high-pressure firearms. A .223 barrel may burst simply because of moisture in the barrel. Run a rod through the barrel of a rifle that has been stored, and get a visual when possible. Barrel obstructions seem to claim more firearms than overly hot ammunition each year.

Firearms do not fire on their own. As long as the shooter performs the proper functions there will be no accidental discharges. All discharges that are unintended are the result of negligence. A person who causes a vehicle accident is guilty of negligent driving; the driver may be charged with simple tort or something more serious when injury is involved. Those who are inattentive, distracted, or incompetent have no business on the firing

Steel gong targets (innovativetargets. net) are excellent training resources. Be certain to respect the recommended setback for safe shooting.

range. When one is firing on the range for practice, the sights are lined up and the trigger is pressed, so a miss isn't acceptable. Neither is unsafe handling. When you begin to work at speed shooting, shooting at distance, and firing self-loading rifles quickly, muzzle discipline and trigger discipline become even more important. The first step is to get training. A certified NRA instructor is a phone call or email away. Absorb the training, and then apply it.

I cannot stress enough how you must understand the difference between shooting at paper and shooting people. Paper targets do not bleed, and a miss isn't serious. You must always be aware of your muzzle, trigger discipline, and backstop. (Whether the gun is loaded or not is immaterial, as all guns must be thought of as always being loaded.) Maximum speed comes with practice, and as we pursue these maximum speed drills we must be aware that *perfect safety* is also demanded as we

During tactical movement, it is especially important not to move with the finger in register.

speed up our practice. Training must be goal-oriented in order for you to progress as a shooter. The primary goal—safety—must never be forgotten. The goal of proficiency at arms is not simply one of marksmanship; that is only one component. Safety and gun handling are equally important. The speed with which a rifle is safely handled and loaded, the ammunition supply replenished, and the rifle made safe are all equally important.

I would not say one firearm is safer than any other, although older bolt-action rifles that rely upon a twist of the bolt out of battery to make the rifle safe give me pause. Unless we are on the stalk for game, or actively involved in a defensive situation, the rifle chamber should be empty, particularly when in storage or at home ready. Those who disagree have attended a different church than mine.

The weight of the trigger press isn't directly related to safety; trigger discipline is what will matter. The weight of the trigger versus the weight of the rifle is not as important as in the case of a handgun. Just the same, we all want a clean, smooth trigger break. A clean break need not be light, but should be smooth enough, and repeatable as well. What is best for the range may not be the best for practical and tactical use. Different types of triggers feel different. A hammer or striker powered by a leaf spring imparts a different break than one powered by a coil spring. While some triggers are a triumph of the technical over the tactical, there are also rifles supplied with good factory triggers. Trigger compression must simply be controllable.

Safety during movement is critical. Ninety-nine percent of the cartridges fired during your lifetime will be fired in training and practice. Like any sport, from biking to mountain climbing, the risk doesn't outweigh the benefits, but must be controlled. The foundation of all types of practical shooting is safe gun handling. You should always be of the mindset that "*All guns are hot, always loaded.*" When you arrive at a firing range, the rifle should not be loaded in the vehicle or on the walk to the firing line, but instead on the firing line/safe area. I have used firing ranges that have only one berm at the end of the firing line, but I prefer the three-sided bay. To explain this type of firing area, imagine a line running through the shooter parallel with the downrange berm. This is the 180-degree line. As long as the muzzle is pointed downrange across this 180-degree line, the shot will travel to one of the berms safely in the event that the shooter accidentally presses the trigger when he doesn't really mean to. (True malfunctions caused by a bad sear, a high primer, or stuck forward firing pin are rare, but do occur.) In such instances, if the muzzle turns up range, there is a real possibility of death or injury.

MOVING

Maneuvering with an army is advantageous, with an undisciplined multitude, most dangerous.

—Sun Tzu

Some do not understand why the military insists that soldiers are able not only to disassemble their rifles, but to do so by touch, blindfolded or in the dark. Absolute familiarity with the rifle is demanded. You should be able to manipulate controls and load and unload the rifle without a visual on the controls. When you are moving, you must keep your eye on the terrain, not the rifle. You must know where the muzzle,

When preparing to fire, the shooter must be familiar with the controls and have the finger off the bang switch.

trigger, and safety are for safety concerns. Stick to a single rifle and learn it thoroughly. The next rifle will be easier. Learning to learn is a constant in every endeavor.

Moving with the Rifle

If you are engaged in team tactics, tactical training, or even hunting with the family, you will be moving with a group of people who are armed. The rifles should be unloaded during movement to the hunting stand. When clearing an area, the rifles are hot. They are loaded. The same safety must be exercised at all times. It is the same as with any team effort.

One member of the team may have a designated chore, or position, that is maintained. Among the most important rules is that the individual moving with the others must maintain visual contact with the person in front of him or her. He or she must be aware of the person to each side and to the immediate rear, but the person in front is the person who would be covered with the rifle in the event of a lapse in muzzle discipline. This person is in the greatest danger. He or she must also maintain proper spacing between team members, so that if one trips and falls the other will not be affected. If you have seen images of a SWAT team about to assault a building, you will note that they maintain distance until they

These professionals are training with the finger off the trigger and practicing all relevant safety cautions (Colt Defense).

actually assault the building. Their muzzle discipline is faultless. As you move with the others, maintain situational awareness. This means you will be aware of other hunters or shooters, and in more serious movement you will be aware of a possible threat. Often you will have been given an individual area of responsibility. When you move, you peel off with the rifle muzzle away from the other shooters.

SAFETY IN THE HOME

The same rules apply to firearm safety in the home. There is no good reason that a number of firearms should be kept loaded around the home. If your threat level is this high, the firearm should be kept on the person. You might have a certain firearm you keep in the room with you at all times. If you do, the Tactical Walls tactical furnishings should be used. They offer a variety of shelves, lamps, and tissue boxes (for example) to disguise firearms in the home setting.

Some years ago, when working to convict and incarcerate a neo-Nazi leader, I had some concern with his active service elements. The action included a rather spectacular spin into the mud by an Oldsmobile Toronado and coverage by *Rolling Stone* magazine. I thought it wise to keep my Colt AR-15 HBAR handier than usual. But during this time, I did not keep the rifle with a round in the chamber. I kept the rifle in the cruiser with the safety off and chamber empty, and I did the same in my home at night. It was the only good rifle I owned and was kept close at hand more than once.

On another occasion, I guarded a government official who had suffered the murder of two family members by a psychotic cousin armed with an AR-15 rifle. While the Colt was ready across my knees, the chamber was empty. It spent the night across a couch while Fran (the official) and I enjoyed coffee and discussions of the future of the town. When the long gun is kept for defense at home ready, it should be kept chamber empty. Only if an immediate threat exists should the rifle be fully loaded and safety on. This could include hunting, clearing an area, or home defense when a threat is imminent. It isn't a problem to quickly manipulate a

Practice removing the magazine and clearing the rifle.

lever-action, bolt-action, or self-loading rifle and make it ready.

Significant practice should be undertaken in quickly loading the rifle and making it ready, as well as in making it safe. As an example, I have guarded family members' farms against predators and have occasionally taken down coyote and feral dogs. In this situation, if I am on a stand, which may mean my back is to the tree and the rifle may be a .32-20 or an AR-15, the chamber is loaded. The hammer must be cocked or the safety moved to fire the rifle. The field of fire is such that the muzzle covers the likely entry point of the stock-killing predator. When the farm-hands are awake and moving, it is time to make the rifle safe.

You must practice removing the magazine, clearing the chamber, and returning the previously chambered round to the magazine, then making

Much of our initial training should be dry-fire with a triple-checked, unloaded rifle. (Battleriflecompany.com)

the rifle safe for carry. If you use a bolt-action rifle or lever-action rifle, then you must get the feel for levering the chambered cartridge out of the chamber and replacing it in the magazine. Most of us will agree the AR-15 is the handiest of rifles to load and unload safely, but other rifles can also be learned with a minimum of effort.

I like to think I have trained the best possible raw material—but raw just the same. I like to speak with tolerance and without insult, but with firmness. Firearm safety is too important to be taken lightly.

CHAPTER TWO

BASIC RIFLE MARKSMANSHIP

During your daily routine you may be on a conference call, checking email, and eating lunch simultaneously. This division of attention is the norm in everyday life. But ask yourself: Are you then truly engaged in any of these activities? On the other hand, you must practice deep focus when learning to fire the rifle properly. Some call it mindfulness. Deep focus, paying attention to your breathing, and considering every action leads to memory retention and situational awareness. You must concentrate on each step in marksmanship. When beginning to learn to shoot—and to shoot well—you must follow the template that has been set down by the best shooters and instructors in the world. You cannot learn this on your own, but there are a variety of resources available. A basic National Rifle Association course is invaluable, followed by personal development that never ends.

There is only one way to learn to shoot. You must understand the fundamentals before you fire your rifle. Long hours of study and dry-fire are essential. I have yet to meet a top contender who was arrogant, humorless, sarcastic, or overinflated, so marksmanship must offer unlimited opportunity for character development. Dry-fire is conducted using a rifle that you have triple-checked—checked three times and removed the magazine, then cleared the chamber three times—in a safe environment. The safe environment may be your home. Dry-fire is achieved by aiming at a small finite target such as an orange paster dot. No one in the home should be in the line of fire in case of a mistake. The backstop should be able to stop a bullet, such as a bullet trap, a bookcase with heavy books, or a brick wall. Learning to hold the rifle, to properly align the sights, and to properly press the trigger is best achieved in conducting dry-fire.

  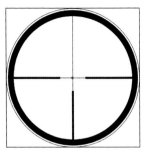

This is the basic sight alignment.   This is the sight picture, which is sight alignment superimposed over the target.   This reticle offers a neat, clean picture. Note the illuminated reticle.

The first rule is to maintain a steady firing position. This position should allow you to properly address the target while maintaining stability. You must aim at the target using the proper sight picture. A front post sight must be centered in the rear sight aperture. An optical sight must have the reticle centered on the target. Sight alignment is finite and always the same.

The hold may be just below the target or dead-on the target, depending upon how the sights are set. No matter what type of rifle you ultimately use, you should begin marksmanship training with iron sights at a modest distance. Beginning with a .22 caliber rifle at 15 yards is ideal. Become proficient at this range, then move to 25 yards. Many of you will be limited to an indoor range, and practice at 15 yards with a .22 at reduced-size targets works well. The concept is simple: aim and fire without disturbing the alignment of the sights on the target. Trigger press may be the most difficult skill to learn, but they are all equally important. Whatever level of proficiency you advance to, marksmanship is the single most important skill after safety. Whether you settle upon a bolt-action .308, a .30-30, a top end AR-15, or a trusted .22, marksmanship must be mastered or the rifle will be underutilized.

This shooter is practicing precision fire from a benchrest.

STEADY FIRING POSITION

As you assume the firing position on the firing line, you will find the benchrest position most useful for initial training. This should be on the benchrest, with your body seated and the rifle cradled on sandbags as you begin. You will spend some time finding a comfortable and stable position. Cheekweld should be maintained. This is placing the cheek to the stock in a manner that presents the eye to the sights. Once this is found, it will take a minimum of time to assume this firing position with the next stop at the range. If you are able to hold the sight picture as the trigger is pressed, you have found a good firing position.

Elements of the Firing Position

Support Hand

The support hand should hold the rifle as far forward as possible for best control. (Be aware of the AR-15 gas block—it gets hot!) When you advance to a standing position, the vee of the thumb and fingers will support the stock. In benchrest fire, the grip need not be tight as the forend is balanced on the support. For offhand fire and in tactical movement, the grip must be as tight as possible.

Rifle Butt Position

It is common to ride the rifle butt too high. The butt should be buried into the pocket of the shoulder. Lean slightly into the butt to reduce recoil. When beginning and when firing a .22, maintain this slight angle and control recoil; the practice will pay off with the .223 and .308 rifles. Too often we grasp the rimfire trainer too lightly during training. Make training serious groundwork for the heavy calibers. The non-firing hand exerts pressure to the rear to ensure the stock is properly placed.

Get a good solid rest against a support. Excellent fire may be done with aperture sights.

Firing Hand

The firing hand will grasp the rifle with the trigger finger in line with the trigger and the thumb alongside the left-hand side of the stock. Do not lay the firing hand thumb alongside the right-side stock with conventional-type rifle stocks. With a pistol grip, the V formed by the thumb and forefinger is the natural

The author is carefully benchresting this lever-action rifle for accuracy. These rifles are often surprisingly accurate for the person willing to master proper technique.

alignment of the firing hand. The trigger finger moves independent of the other fingers. Always be certain that sympathetic motion of the non-firing fingers is controlled as the trigger finger moves to the rear. This motion is called milking the trigger, and erodes trigger control. The elbow helps the shoulders remain level. The elbow may be used as a tripod when properly aligned with the shoulders. When standing, the elbow may not offer support but helps guide the rifle toward the target.

Cheekweld

Cheekweld, or cheek-to-stock contact, is important. The cheek is held on the rifle so that a natural line of sight is maintained between the eyes and the front sight, and continuing to the target. The neck must be relaxed. If the neck is compressed, blood flow may be affected and thus the shooter's vision may become blurred. The neck is relaxed, allowing the cheek to fall naturally onto the stock. Relentlessly practice this in dry-fire until the action of cheekweld becomes automatic. Without consistency, the firing position will not be accu-

rate, and without comfort the firing position will not be consistent. When the shooter establishes a proper cheekweld, proper eye relief becomes automatic. The slight changes in eye relief in different firing positions will not affect the shooter as much if you have the proper cheekweld. Have a visual on the rifle sights or reticule as you maintain cheekweld.

The author has fired, eyes are on the sights, a spent case is in the air, and the trigger finger returning to the trigger; accurate rapid fire is possible with the lever-action rifle.

Bones versus Muscles

When using the rifle, the bones—rather than the muscles—should be used as support. Muscles tire; bones do not. When assuming a kneeling firing position, or any position that uses a type of support such as the barricade or firing from cover, if the bones are lined up properly to support the rifle the shooter will be able to properly keep the rifle steady. Muscle fatigue and tremor result in sight wobble.

DRIVING THE GUN

When you are in the natural firing position, the front sight will tend to be off the target. The sight must be driven toward the target and kept there. The aiming point must be maintained. After firing you will maintain your firing position and grip. This is known as follow-through. Follow-through is simple: maintain the proper hold on the rifle after it fires. This is important in properly managing the rifle. You should spend as much time as needed in assuming the firing position. Once you feel competent to move to standing, kneeling, and prone firing positions, be certain that you engage in dry-fire and learning positioning first, before you attempt live fire exercises.

When you are confident in your ability to hold the rifle properly, you will learn to align the sights. The rifle must be aligned with the target exactly the same for each shot. When using iron sights the rear sight may be a bit blurry, but the front post must be sharp and clear. The target must also be blurry. The eye cannot focus on three planes at once; the front post is the most important focus point. (An advantage of optical sights is that the focal planes are reduced to one aiming point; but you should master iron sights

This young captain is strong and can shoot benchrest groups pretty easily. Aperture sights work for him.

first.) Keep the front sight in focus. Use the six o'clock hold, placing the front sight at the bottom of the bullseye. It is important to keep the front sight on the same spot for each trigger press. An aperture sight must keep the front post in the center of the "ghost ring" rear sight. Open or leaf rear sights demand the sight be held in the center of the rear leaf. At this point let me repeat an old axiom: front sight, front sight, front sight! If you maintain focus on the front sight, errors at longer range are much less likely. Never allow yourself to shift focus to the rear sight.

TARGET

The sight picture is attained after you have the proper sight alignment. The correct sight picture will include the front and rear sights and the target. The sight picture is the superimposition of the front post over the target or aiming point. The actual aiming point will vary with short and long range, even if the rifle is fitted with an optical sight, but the principles used in initial short- to medium-range training will apply.

Part of the marksman's challenges is that rifle shooting is more deliberate than handgun shooting in long-range fire. Breath control must be understood. When engaging targets at long range, breath control is essential. When the shooter has exhaled and the air has left his lungs is the proper time for the trigger press. You do not hold your breath, as that incites muscle tremor. You exhale and relax *before* you pull the trigger. Trigger control and breath control go hand in hand. The trigger press cannot disturb the aim of the rifle. A jerking movement of the trigger finger may move the sight off center. The trigger press is always smooth and straight to the rear. When addressing moving targets at short range, the trigger press is compressed into a much shorter amount of time, but smooth and straight to the rear.

The shooter should be aware that there are things that may cause the shooter to jerk the trigger or flinch. These things include muzzle blast and recoil.

Sighting in, and final, adjustments are done carefully. Read the paper.

I find that most shooters find muzzle blast more disconcerting than recoil, at least at the .223 level. While we always wear eye protection and hearing protection, both muzzle blast and flash take some acclimation. You must be aware of what is going on when you press the trigger. While flinch or involuntary movement of the hand is common, many shooters do not realize that they are also tensing their shoulder at times

This young shooter is taking a careful shot. He understands that the only important shot is the one he is firing.

when firing. The shooter may not realize he is doing this, but the effect is detrimental to accurate fire. The miss may not be slight; the paper may be missed at 100 yards, and the groups not groups at all but spatterings.

Trigger Control

The pad of the trigger finger is placed on the face of the trigger between the tip and first joint of the finger. The fingertip alone will not have sufficient leverage for proper trigger control. The trigger is straight to the rear. The firing pin must strike forward without disturbing the sight alignment or sight picture. You may take as much time as you need to master the break. Always remember that the shot being fired is the most important shot of the day. Every shot is important, and is a separate event. A string of shots are

Different rifles require a different hold, but basic skills are the same.

several carefully controlled shots, with equal importance allotted to each. As you progress as a shooter, recovery time and follow-up shots will be addressed. But first, master the trigger. As an example, when my son, Alan, was very young he would hang on the trigger so long I thought he had gone to sleep on the bench! But he reached a point of not missing, and eventually became the best shot I know. When he fires, he compresses the trigger straight to the rear, and carefully, but he does so more quickly when speed shooting. A good benchmark when you begin to fire off the benchrest is to fire a shot every five seconds. If you feel you have made a mistake with the sights or trigger, do not break the shot but relax and try to control the shot again. Once you become accustomed to the drill and become a good shot, you will be able to properly break the trigger within a second. Some shooters firing rapid fire at multiple targets at close range can fire accurately much faster. The trigger must not be milked to the left or right but pressed to the rear. The firing finger must not contact the frame at any point, but only contact the trigger.

Firing Offhand

And old saying is that precision demands lubrication. This simply means *lots of practice*. I have taught quite a few shooters in offhand rifle shooting, and in the end the dedication of the shooter means as much as the skill of the instructor. I have never experienced firsthand the evils of great wealth, but I have enjoyed the satisfaction of a job well done and a student who in time surpassed the instructor's ability. In hunting and personal defense, shooting offhand fire is the most likely to be demanded by the occasion. In personal defense, you will be facing those who are neither active parishioners nor candidates for membership in the Knights of Columbus. You may find your-self boarding at the morgue if you do not get your hit and get it quickly. I have witnessed astounding performance with the rifle, mostly from military men. I have also seen serious hunters who have performed well in offhand fire. In benchrest accuracy we have a standard for both the rifle and the shooter. A few shooters using a quality rifle and good ammunition reach a standard of a three-shot group in 1–2 inches at 100 yards. Some will shoot right up to the rifle's capability. At 100 yards, offhand, a good standard that is a perennial is to hit a paper plate three times in less than a minute offhand at 100 yards.

This is the best shot we know controlling his rifle. His form is ideal.

The forward grip allows excellent control of the rifle, but must be learned properly to deliver good accuracy.

When you achieve this goal, you are a credible offhand shot. After firing small groups at the gridiron range this sounds easier than it is. The best of the shooter's core competency is demanded. A well set up AR-15 with an ergonomic stock and good sights is among the easiest of rifles to use to achieve this goal. The .30-30 Winchester isn't out of the running. And the shooter must develop the necessary skill sets.

Tips

Control that trigger! When standing offhand no matter how good the support, you are more likely to pull the rifle off the target due to a poor trigger break. This is where offhand dry-fire practice will pay off. Hold the rifle firmly, but do not invite muscle tremor. Increase pressure on the rifle until your muscles tremble, then back off and you will have your correct hold. It is simple, but finding the perfect balance eludes many shooters. Stand with the left side of the body bladed toward the target. Feet should be a shoulder's width apart. Keep the rifle butt settled into the shoulder. The support arm should be bladed down and supported by your body. The elbow should be against the rib cage. Shooters with long arms may find the rifle resting against the hip in good measure. A slight forward lean is good. The support hand should support the rifle. When you advance to rapid fire you will effect a different stance, but for target shooting and a good beginning this stance will work. A bit of wobble is expected, there is nothing you can do. Execute the proper trigger press and breath control.

By cinching up tightly with the rifle sling, excellent offhand stability is possible.

When beginning this drill, your results will likely not be good unless you have invested considerable time in dry-fire. Even so, offhand fire takes some time to master. The results are relative and will never equal benchrest scores, but they are useful and will provide game taking and life-saving accuracy. A cornerstone technique for offhand fire is proper use of the rifle sling. The sling is capable of welding the rifle and the shooter together. The sling keeps the shooting position rigid. The military sling is a basic design but features a loop, keepers, hooks or frogs, and setting holes. All need a break-in when new. For tactical use, I have used both the Blackhawk! and Specter Gear slings.

Begin by moving the sling high on your arm. The triceps will support the sling and keep it in place. The sling should run from the center of the arm, then around the back of the wrist and hand without cutting into the wrist, picking up a pulse, and becoming too tight. A 0.5-inch clockwise twist in the sling end before attachment of the swivel will allow it to pass around the side of the wrist and back. Maintain a straight and comfortable wrist position. It is important that the hand fit snugly against the hand stop on the sling. With the AR-15 rifle, the Specter Sling and the Blue Force Vickers sling are recommended. Blackhawk! offers an extensive line of good slings as well.

Get the sling tight and control the rifle, and surprisingly accurate fire may be exhibited offhand.

CHAPTER THREE

CHOOSING A RIFLE

BEST FOR MONEY, BEST FOR MERIT

Rifles are not inexpensive in their best renditions. While I urge the reader to purchase a quality rifle, I would not necessarily purchase a high-end rifle the first go 'round. But certainly, a quality rifle is the best first rifle. Most of us move to a different choice after the initial purchase, but there are others who cling to that first choice. As an example, I have owned several AR-15 rifles but the Colt remains my go-to primary rifle. Whatever the rifle type, there are considerations that must be addressed. If you are new to rifle shooting, then your first rifle might be a .22 rimfire.

.22 Long Rifle

Ammunition is inexpensive, available, and accurate. A good quality .22 caliber rifle, such as the Ruger 10/22, will not be outgrown. Rather, it will be appreciated throughout its useful life. Small game hunting, informal target practice, and even home defense are roles for which the .22 caliber rifle may

The Ruger 10/22 takedown is quite simply one of the finest, if not the finest, rifle ever made in this caliber.

shine. Bolt-action rifles are widely available and so are lever-action rifles. If you have done an honest appraisal, and you believe that a bolt-action rifle and long-range use is your goal, then a quality bolt-action rifle may be a good start. However, I use many action types and do not particularly feel that that moving from the bolt-action .22 to a self-loading .223 is a great challenge. The simplicity and reliability of the Ruger 10/22 self-loader is such that there really isn't much competition.

10/22

The Ruger may be had with the classic lines of a wood stock, or with modern black tactical accoutrements. Other affordable choices include the basic lever-action Henry rifle, a surprisingly accurate firearm. The .22 Long Rifle is a versatile cartridge that is a great all-around beginner's rifle. This should be one's first rifle, ideally. For some of us the need for a centerfire rifle is more

The author fitted a LaserMax to this 10/22. A good kit!

Old and worn Ruger with Skinner sights. A workhorse.

pressing, and our first rifle is often a centerfire. We need a defense or varmint rifle right now! This isn't the handicap some would suppose, given proper training. I have trained many shooters who have never fired the .22, but instead have jumped right into the .223 with success. It depends on one's level of dedication and level of training.

When choosing a rifle, you must consider the mission. This is a tough one for some of us. If the mission is squirrel hunting, the .22 LR is the ideal forager. If the purpose is personal defense, a lever-action Brooklyn Special might be considered, or the AR-15 rifle. We have to look at the rifles with a clear eye and consider what our needs are. We also need to take into consideration the amount of training and range time we are willing to dedicate to the rifle.

The 10/22 Takedown comes apart easily and goes back together with a minimum of effort, yet retains its accuracy and sight setting.

For personal defense and survival roles, the AR-15 rifle will often be the best choice. Before choosing a rifle in an alternate caliber to the .223 Remington, I would carefully consider ammunition supply; more about that in the chapter on ammunition choice. Just be certain that you will be able to feed the beast on a regular schedule. A balance of power and accuracy must be considered. If you like to hunt coyote at 200–300 yards, you need a tighter rifle than the bargain basement special at the pawn shop. You also have to look yourself straight in the eye and determine if you are truly willing to properly maintain the rifle. There is a reason the Winchester lever-action rifle is treasured in harsh climates! The AR-15 is a reliable rifle, but if you do not regularly clean and lubricate it, and fire cases of dirty ammunition in it, this rifle will not be long lived nor reliable. Some shooters begin with the .223

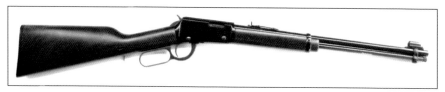

The Henry .22 is a great all-around rifle.

and move to the .308 AR-10, which is understandable, but most keep their .223 as well. I think that deciding to own two rifles comes *after* you have learned the first rifle and find a limitation in it.

If a rifle is intended for precision long-range fire it will probably have a long barrel. The rifle will be heavy. Precision fire has many meanings. My personal Remington 700 .308 rifle with an 18-inch barrel is as accurate as I will ever need at a long 150 yards, and useful to 200 yards. But if the primary objective is long-range fire, common sense tells you that the balance of accuracy and maximum muzzle velocity favors the longer barrel. Rigidity favors the *stiffer* barrel, not necessarily the longer barrel, but that is an advanced discussion. The standard AR-15 carbine is most useful for home defense and area defense. But if varmint hunting or deer-sized game is what you have in mind, you may wish to invest in the longer rifle. If personal defense inside the home is your primary consideration, and you are not interested in the shooting sports or hunting, a good quality pistol-caliber carbine may be worthwhile options. They are not rifles, and are limited in what they can accomplish, but within their narrow mission profile they are one choice.

At this point you have noticed that I am not spelling out the rifle *you* should purchase. I cannot do that for you. I may enumerate qualities that the rifle should have, but only *you* know which rifle will make *you* happy and suit *your* needs. I can tell you that some rifles are more comfortable to fire off the benchrest than others. There is no rifle that is more ergonomic than the AR-15 for all-around use. A lot depends upon the ammunition and sighting equipment used, which we will cover later.

Personal enjoyment means much. As one example of my own personal enjoyment and practical use, some time ago I owned a Howa .223 rifle with Nikon scope. With a heavy barrel and excellent trigger, the rifle turned in 0.5-inch groups with the Black Hills 52-grain MATCH loading at 100 yards,

This Winchester lever-action rifle is not only a good performer; the history and pride of ownership are priceless.

Before venturing into AR-15 territory, ask yourself if you need one, then get ready for a lot of fun.

sometimes a little less. I seldom fired the rifle, but when I did my job with the proper hold and trigger press, the results were always the same. At the same time, I owned a Colt HBAR. The Leupold scope was more ordinary and the trigger heavier. From the same benchrest with the same ammunition, the Colt delivered 0.9-inch to 1.25-inch 100-yard groups. With the Black Hills Ammunition 60-grain JSP, a three-shot 100-yard group might break 1.25 inches. I was on a tight budget with two children in high school and simply could not justify both rifles. I kept the Colt. In practical terms, there was nothing the Colt could not do at 200 yards that the Howa could. That is why a quality AR-15 is such a versatile rifle. At 300–400 yards, the Howa would have been a different story; but that is not what I needed.

Expense

A rifle isn't a throwaway; it is an investment. The rifle should be of good quality, but not so expensive that its loss or replacement would be a hardship. A 22-caliber rifle is inexpensive largely because the cartridge offers little pressure and the steel isn't very hard in these rifles. Aluminum is heavily used. The modern push feed centerfire bolt-action rifle is often quite inexpensive, even when topped with a mid-quality rifle scope. You must make an honest appraisal of your budget when considering a purchase. It is common to see used rifles in a shop that are the result of someone's impulse buy, and a subsequent fast resell when the credit card bill came due. You can lose a lot—typically 40 percent of the purchase price—when making a poor decision on a first rifle. We all have budgets, some larger than others. I would recommend going with the rifle you really believe you will prefer, right from the

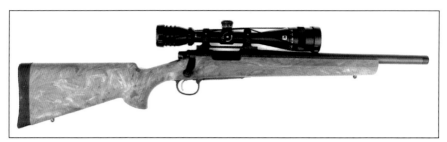

The Remington 700 .308 is the author's favorite bolt gun. Its strong suit is accuracy.

beginning. If you want an AR-15, an inexpensive AR will be a better companion than the SKS rifle you might be able to afford. Remember, when you trade you are going to lose 40 percent off the retail price. Sometimes used guns are a bargain, sometimes not, but they can be hard to find in some calibers. I find many to be overvalued. If you feel that the SKS, AK-47, or Ruger Mini-14 fills your bill, then by all means go with your personal choice.

As an example, my friend Ross, a retired US Army Major, chose the Ruger Mini-14 as his go-to rifle. He was bored with the AR after twenty years and wanted something different. Ross was well pleased with his only rifle. There are good choices if you want a useful rifle and the preference is for reliability. The SKS may use a good scope mount, holds ten rounds of powerful ammunition, and an example in good order is reasonably accurate. This is a minimalist rifle with a good reputation. The SKS is fun to shoot. Without starting a debate, the SKS is often more accurate than the AK-47 rifle, although the newest AK-47 rifles will be tighter than the average rifle of a few decades ago. The SKS is simple, a good truck gun, and can be a lot of fun. As for bolt-action rifles, the Mosin–Nagant, Mauser, and Lee Enfield are choices that are sometimes affordable. They have been creeping up or exploding in price, and may not be as good a buy as they once were. The Nagant is long and heavy, but is a decent shooter that is easy to service. The Mauser rifle features a controlled feed design that is among the single most reliable military rifles ever fielded. My personal favorite for firing from the bench and obtaining excellent accuracy is the .30-06 Springfield 1903 or the 1903A3. They are also increasingly expensive. For tactical use, the greatest bolt-action rifle of the two World Wars is the British Lee Enfield. With an action that isn't overly affected by dirt and grime, and a fast handling bolt action as well as a ten-round magazine, the Lee Enfield stands alone as a model of tactical

Sometimes nothing puts a smile on her face like a pistol-caliber carbine.

Mossberg offers a number of excellent all-around rifles at a fair price.

effectiveness. Both the Mauser and the Lee Enfield are still in use in India and the Middle East as issue to palace guards, police, and the like.

The First AR-15 Rifle

Quite a few shooters get the bug and jump into an AR-15 rifle as their first rifle. It is ergonomic, reliable if maintained, and readily available. Parts are available in the thousands, and so is ammunition. If you do not like the rifle, it isn't hard to trade up or down. When you look at the field, the choice can be daunting. I do not know how many makers or assemblers of AR-15 rifles there are, but there are many. I came up with twenty, counting my fingers and toes, and then stopped. I am certain I missed a few. I have shot ARs from Colt, Bushmaster, CORE, Daniel Defense, Sturm Ruger, and Smith & Wesson,

The dirt-tough SKS, above, will solve a lot of problems, such as area defense and predator control. The Daniel rifle, below, has more finesse.

The plain Joe Mini-14 rifle is never a bad choice.

This Ruger Tactical Model has been purchased by a number of agencies. This is a great all-around rifle.

This synthetic stock Ruger with muzzle brake is among the most rugged rifles in the world.

all with excellent results. I have tested Battle Rifle Company rifles at *Gun Tests* magazine with further good results. I am certain some of the makers are assemblers and practically everyone outsources one part or the other, even if it is the stocks and hardware. How do you choose the best rifle without ten years of experience? Asking friends who shoot a lot is one good resource. Ask a three-gun competitor what holds up. A good quality AR-15 should not be a parts gun. The receiver and upper should match, and so should the barrel. Just because the frame says Rock River Arms, as an example, it all may not be so. These patchwork rifles do not always perform well. The looser the tolerances of a rifle, the more slop in the parts and the greater the chance of eccentric wear and malfunctions. Low-priced versions from a major maker may work okay. The original Smith & Wesson Sport doesn't have a forward assist or dust cover. Mine has been a great shooter from day one. It is accurate at 100 yards with Black Hills Ammunition 60-grain A-Max load. I added a Hiperfire duty trigger and it has worked out well. I have picked up cheap rifles and found that the stock rattled when shook, and that the rifle was generally disagreeable. Such rifles also have cheaper internals. While some quality rifles do not have chrome-lined bores, I prefer them. I break open the rifle and check to see if the carrier key is properly staked. If it isn't, the rest of the rifle probably isn't going to be better than third class either. When it comes to many types of firearms, I look for good used firearms at gun shops and pawnshops. When it comes to AR-15s, however, I try to buy a new gun. If I am considering buying a used AR-15 rifle, I give it a thorough inspection. People tend to shoot these rifles a lot and also like to fiddle with them. So, with that warning, while you may find a good deal on a used AR-15, a new AR-15 rifle is the safer choice. More on this in the next chapter.

CHAPTER FOUR

AR-15 RIFLES

W̶e touched upon the AR-15 rifle in the previous chapter, but this rifle is worth an in-depth look. You should own at least one example of the Armalite design, America's rifle. I did my research before buying, and I am happy with the rifles I own. When I purchased my AR-15, Colt was the only choice, and I certainly did not go wrong. Today, of course, there

If you are going to build your own, use a good foundation. This is the author's Spikes Tactical rifle.

are innumerable options. Some are made to perform at the top end, while others are made cheaply and perform accordingly. I have experienced excellent results with Colt, Ruger, Smith & Wesson, and Daniel Defense. I have been impressed with CORE15 rifles, and found Bushmaster acceptable. You will have to judge for yourself on individual rifles, and use the build quality and performance of proven rifles as a baseline. The baseline in caliber is 5.56mm or .223 Remington, though I would choose 5.56mm for my first AR. As a personal defense rifle, you will probably never need to change this caliber. The .308 adds more expense, greater recoil, and more power. While some of us may have no problem handling the .308, I think that a new shooter should concentrate on the affordable, low-recoil .223. If you buy a poor rifle, your entry into the shooting world will have a much different character. Purchase a proven rifle and you'll be pleased with the performance.

There are variations on the rifle. The M4 type, with a 16-inch barrel, is by far the most common. In contrast, the M16 type has a 20-inch barrel. For

Do you need a SBR? If so, the SIG is a first-class choice.

fast handling, personal defense, and small-game hunting, I prefer the 16-inch barrel. Gas impingement is also the way to go for a first rifle. Some shooters prefer piston systems, but all piston systems are not alike, while the AR-15 is Mil-Spec and will accept a myriad of parts. A good rifle may be had for eight to twelve hundred dollars, while a decent rifle such as the Core15 may be had for even less. I would also choose iron sights on a first rifle, for reasons mentioned in the marksmanship section.

You need a rifle that stresses the good attributes of the AR-15 rifle. These features include precise engineering, durability, and practical accuracy. For hunting, the rifle offers a fast follow-up if needed. For personal defense, home defense, or area defense, nothing works as well as a good AR-15. The rifle is a great ranch rifle as well. The only question is whether the caliber is adequate for the task at hand. With the viability of modern, highly developed .223 loads and rifles chambered in heavier calibers, this question has been answered. The AR rifle is primarily made of polymer and

This is a precision rifle on the AR platform. It doesn't get any better.

Do you need a .308? If you do, consider the Smith & Wesson AR-10.

The Mission First Tactical stock from Brownells is at the top of our list.

aluminum, with aluminum or polymer magazines. This means the rifle is tough. There is little to rust, so fewer things can go wrong. As for reliability, I maintain my rifle regularly, but even those shooters who do not keep the rifle maintained to a gold standard will find the AR-15 reliable. Get a chrome-lined bore; do not go cheap on that. Again, ask yourself the question, "What will I be doing with the rifle?" The size issue really revolves around the magazines. What will fit in the magazine well? The rifle has been chambered to a number of interesting cartridges, including the 6.8 SPC, .300 Blackout, and .450 Bushmaster.

An option is the AR-10, which is a different rifle with much the same handling. The AR-10 is famously chambered in .308 Winchester, but may be chambered for the .338 Federal or .300 WSM. The possibilities an advanced shooter has available with upper receivers and calibers is interesting too. For example, a .223 for home defense may easily be converted to a .450 for deer

Hogue offers excellent accessories for the AR-15 rifle.

A specialized choice for the AR-15 rifle is the .300 Blackout chambering.

or hogs. I personally prefer owning two rifles instead of a number of conversions, but just the same, the versatility is there for those who want it.

BUILDING AR-15 RIFLES

That said, I would be cautious about buying self-built rifles and parts guns, as many are deficient in one manner or another. Personal research also uncovered some excellent rifles, built by a number of friends. Again, the key is to define the mission. It is important to choose which upper receiver you want to use. The AR-15 A1 is the original, non-removable carrying handle. If you are

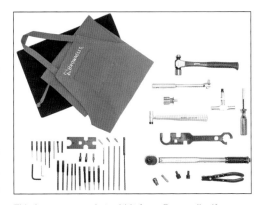

This is an armorer's tool kit from Brownells. If you build the AR rifle, you must have it.

building a retro AR-15 with an M16 look, this is a good choice. And while it isn't optic ready, you are not going to knock the sights out of zero! This is the least versatile and least popular choice. The AR-15 A2 assembly has superior, fully adjustable sights. For shooting matches and general personal defense use, I find this example a good all-around setup. However, the AR-15 A3, with

Picatinny rail, is the better and more versatile choice. You may mount a fixed carrying handle or the removable type on this rail, or you may mount an optical sight. The Picatinny rail type or the AR-15 flattop are usually chosen for those intending to mount optics. Iron sights or back-up sights may be used. Begin by choosing the upper assembly. For good quality parts, I recommend Brownells. They demand quality from their suppliers and possibly have the greatest selection in the world. Pick a 16- or 20-inch barrel, standard, free-floating or KeyMod rail and your choice of bolt carrier, and you are in business.

This kit, from Brownells, contains quality parts and makes an AR build go smoothly.

I have enjoyed excellent results with a 20-inch upper that I often use on my AR-556 rifle. This upper is from Del-Ton. When I wish to wring the most from a combination of the shooter and ammunition, I use this

The Wheeler Delta Series kit from Brownells is for advanced builders. That is, you and I with quality parts.

upper. You will need the proper tools to assemble the rifle. Bite the bullet and buy these from Brownells. The proper tools will pay a big dividend in putting together your version of America's rifle. When you consider the lower receiver, this is the part that the trigger guard, trigger assembly, magazine catch, bolt stop and bolt release, pistol grip, butt stock, and other parts attach to.

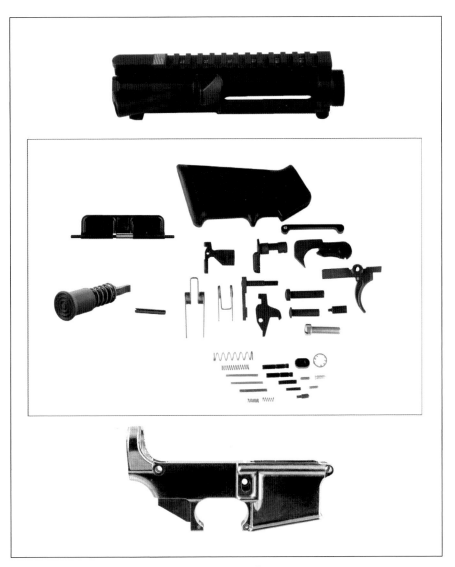

Just about everything needed may be found at Brownells.com

There are few choices in this configuration. All trigger guards fit all receivers, in my experience. Some makers have a forge flash protrusion under the trigger, and some are rougher between the receiver extension and the pistol grip. Others have a noticeable flash line around the lips of the magazine well. The transition in lines isn't as smooth with some receivers as others. I have used Spikes Tactical receivers and build parts with excellent results.

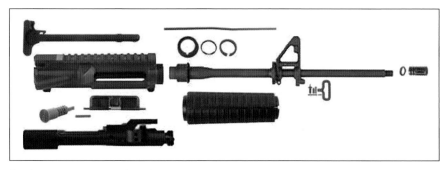

This is the upper build kit from Brownells. Start with quality when building a rifle.

Testing Rifles

In these few pages, I am going to evaluate a number of good quality AR-15 rifles. While space, time, finances, and ammunition considerations would never allow testing every AR-15 contender, this section will give you an idea of the performance of the various rifles.

Beretta ARX100

This isn't really an AR-15, but it is close. Mechanically, this rifle is more like the AR 180 Beretta. As far as reliability is concerned, these are faultless rifles. They are low maintenance and simple to maintain. The ARX100 is the civilian version of Beretta's ARX160 military rifle. The ARX uses new materials and strict

The author found the Beretta ARX reliable, but not superior to the AR-15 rifle.

quality control, with attention to detail and cost control resulting in a price tag just shy of two thousand dollars but available for much less from certain dealers. The barrel, manufactured in the Beretta facility in Maryland, is a Nitride-treated 16-inch tube with a 1:7 twist rate. The barrel was designed to be easily switched when burned out. This allows conversion to such calibers as the 6.8 and .300 Blackout; but until we see the kits available I reserve comment. Beretta is simply trying to meet demand for the rifle at the moment. The ARX100 features a unique design that lets you change brass ejection on demand from right to left. This makes the ARX100 a truly ambidextrous rifle, with excellent interchangeability and ambi-options.

The selector controls and magazine release are ambidextrous units. There is even an emergency magazine

The author's grandson in rapid fire with the Beretta. It is controllable.

release. If the magazine release does not function correctly, another release just in front of the trigger guard makes for a total of three magazine release buttons! The third lever is a lock rather than a button. It is more like the AK-47 than the AR-15 type release, while the primary release is a close copy of the AR-15.

Unlike the AR-15, the charging handle on the ARX100 reciprocates with the bolt. Therefore, it is easy to simply grasp the bolt-mounted handle and give it a tug. To change the ejected cartridge's path from one side to the other, a bullet nose is inserted into an opening just to the rear of the receiver. This lets you control ejection. There are two extractors, and this cross bolt activates one or the other. There are no dust covers. This may be debated at length, and it is what it is; when being used, cocked and ready for action, the rifle bolt will be exposed. The receiver is of modern impact resistant polymer, and features a rail for mounting optics ranging from a red dot to a dedicated long-range optic. The ARX100 is also supplied with flip-up battle sights. There is nothing revolutionary about these sights; they are credible tools and are calibrated for the 62-grain NATO Green Tip. The front post is the usual rotat-

ing post. The rear sight is a dial aperture and wheel. Different apertures are used at different ranges. This is a good design that proved practical in range testing. The trigger is a typical, military type that does not win over any target shooters, yet breaks clean and does the business. When carrying the rifle, there are four sling slots for the

The modular Beretta rifle is easily field stripped.

supplied sling. The stock is adjustable for length-of-pull and may be folded for easy storage and carry.

Range firing was uneventful. There were no surprises. The Beretta sailed through 240 rounds of Federal Green Tip FMJ ammunition without a single failure to feed, chamber fire, or eject. The rifle was not lubricated; Beretta says it will run dry. It did. I fired it again at two later range sessions for a total of 890 rounds. The feel is different than the AR-15 and the polymer receiver takes some getting used to. Just the same, there are those who felt the recoil was lighter than the AR-15. This may be due to the absence of the buffer tube shuffling. The polymer receiver was easier to hang onto than a sharp-edged quad rail, yet the rifle has plenty of rail for mounting equipment. The rifle was test fired at 50 yards. The limits of iron sights made it unwise to attempt a comparison of accuracy at 100 yards. With the Black Hills 55-grain FMJ, several groups were fired at 50 yards that averaged 2 inches; a few went a little less. I am used to the AR-15, but also used to the Winchester .30-30 and many other rifles. The ARX100, in my opinion, isn't as accurate as the best AR-15 rifles. Magazine compatibility with the AR-15 isn't perfect. The magazines with an overtravel stop stub will not work with the ARX100. Some will find the side folder stock advantageous. Overall, it is a good rifle that features faultless reliability. It is more like the AR 180 than the AR-15, and unless you "just have to be different," there are better choices for a lot less cash.

CMMG M4

This is an entry level rifle that fits the basic M4 description. The rifle was proofed with Brownells magazines and Black Hills FMJ ammunition. Most of the firing was done in combat-type drills, quickly addressing man-sized targets at 25, 50, and 100 yards. The sights are good; however, the sight radius is shorter than a KeyMod-type rail gun. The handguard is just fine for most shooting. After all, the AR-15 rifle does not kick much. All of the good points of the AR-15 rifle—fast handling, light recoil, rapid fire hits on target,

When all are compared, the best shot we know prefers the AR-15.

and reliability—are demonstra-
ble in the CMMG rifle. During
the test my son went prone and
homed in on the 100-yard
target. Results were good, but he
did not like the design of the
folding stock. The pointed butt
plate isn't as stable as the flat
butt plate he prefers. The stock
of the CMMG had play, which

Getting on target fast with a CMMG carbine.

varies from stock to stock in the AR-15. There is nothing wrong with the
stock's function, and it is better than some we have tested. After the initial
workout, I found the CMMG to be a reliable rifle, with no stoppages. Accuracy at 50 yards from a solid rest was average, with most groups around
2 inches. The rifle does what it is designed to do. The stock could have been
better. The CMMG cost less than better rifles. There are other inexpensive
AR-15 rifles; this is a good one.

Battle Rifle Company's BR4

The appearance of the rifle and the handguard give the impression of a
longer rifle, but this isn't true. Only the long muzzle brake makes the rifle
¾-inch longer than the M4 standard. The BR4 is as lively in the hand as
any rifle. While the trigger is heavy, it is smooth and reset is rapid. The
Battle Rifle Company forend receives high marks. It is light enough but
comfortable on firing, and allows many options in mounting combat
lights. At the other end of the rifle the buttstock, from Mission First Tactical, received high marks for its release, which I find the superior type, and
for superior rigidity. The flat of the Battle Rifle Company stock is a welcome
improvement. For fifty dollars, you may upgrade any AR-15; the Battle
Rifle Company rifle is good to go as it is. The plated bolt carrier group is an
advantage in a hard-use rifle. To test absolute accuracy, a Nikon M-223
rifle scope was fitted. The rifle had sailed through several hundred FMJ
loads at short to medium range. At a long 100 yards, the Black Hills
Ammunition 77-grain OTM printed 1.1 inches, with some groups a bit
tighter and some a bit larger. This is good kit. I can manage a heavy but
smooth trigger off the bench, but firing off the hind legs demands a better
trigger action for real accuracy.

Colt M4

The Colt AR-15 has seen wide police and military use, and remains the rifle with the greatest service record. Some decades ago I kept a Colt HBAR in the police cruiser, carefully maintained the rifle, and never had cause to replace it. The Colt challenged me to be all I could be, and I enjoyed firing the rifle. Today, I

The Colt AR-15 is a great all-around rifle. Note the rifle is already back on target while a case is still in the air.

most often deploy a shorter carbine version of the AR-15. Among my favorites is the rifle covered in this section. It is a personal rifle, not a loaner, and that means I have tested it until I trust it. It is good enough to ride with. Colt's M4A1 is a civilian version of the SOCOM carbine. The primary difference is that there is no fully automatic option. The rifle is immensely appealing to Colt fans and to anyone in need of a reliable, accurate, and effective AR-15 rifle. The rifle is well appointed with excellent battle sights, a modern forend with plenty of rail space, and excellent ergonomics. The new rail design is supposed to help dissipate heat more efficiently. While I did not test the rifle to the extent the military has, I was able to fire my semiautomatic rifle until it smoked. The rifle is set up with the modern adjustable stock, post front sight, and a remarkably easy-to-use rear sight. Rather than rotating a wheel for range adjustment, the rear sight is click adjustable for yardage. However, the shortest range setting was 200 yards. The rifle fired high at 100 yards despite my best efforts.

The rifle features a modern forend with quick detachable sling attachments as well as the standard rail for use with lasers and lights. I have fitted a LaserMax green laser to the rail for close range use. The rails accommodate anything from an under-the-barrel light to a modern red dot above the barrel. The slots are numbered. This allows a degree of confidence in the zero when returning a tool to the rail. When handling the rifle, the four-position stock allows a wide range of adjustment for each shooter. The barrel is chrome lined. The bolt, carrier, ejection port, and other parts are familiar to AR-15 shooters, and the rifle is well made of good material. Trigger and hammer pins are 0.0154 inch for reference. The bolt is well finished and the gas keys are properly staked. Why some makers still refuse to properly stake gas keys is beyond me, perhaps for the reason they do not chrome line the barrel. They are getting by as cheaply as possible. The chrome-lined barrel features a 1:7 barrel twist. This is optimum for the present 62-grain Green Tip service load. However, the rifle is accurate with loads from 55 grains to 77 grains. The barrel begins at 0.640 inch and it is 0.0750 inches in diameter at the gas block. The sights are the usual front post and rear aperture. However, the rear sight features a single aperture and a drum that may be rolled for adjustment for the service load to well past 500 yards. The rifle is all AR-15, and anyone familiar with the type will be able to get the measure of the Colt in good order, as far as handling, loading, firing, and maintaining the rifle are concerned. An advantage of this rifle over most AR-15 rifles is that the safety lever is ambidextrous. It isn't difficult for a left-handed shooter to manipulate the magazine release with the forefinger, but the safety is more difficult to engage. The Colt M4A1 neatly solves the problem of left-handed use. When firing the carbine, I was careful to use the hand forward grip that makes the AR-15 so fast and effective. I used primarily Winchester 55-grain FMJ loads in this evaluation, as well as the Magpul PMAG. I used both the Gen 2 and the Gen 3 Magpul magazines, as well as the Gen3 with cartridge counter window and overtravel insertion stop. All functioned ideally. The magazines never gave cause for any concern, locked in as designed, and fell away when the magazine release was pressed.

By keeping the hand close to the muzzle, the rifle is controlled in rapid movement. While the rifle is more stable with this hold, the real advantage is in speed and rapid movement. The Colt showed its heritage, giving excellent results in rapid fire at man-sized targets at 25, 50, and 100 yards. Minute-of-angle work wasn't attempted at that time and I fired the rifle until the forend smoked. The Colt sights were delivered sighted high, so some Kentucky elevation was involved, but once the sights were reset things went smoothly. The Winchester USA ball ammunition was expended without a single stutter. After a cleaning session and lubricating the rifle, three hundred rounds showed no signs of eccentric wear. The next session was slower paced, with time taken to properly sight the rifle. It was so much fun to fire such a great rifle I had made a dent in my .223 reserves! I was lucky enough to have obtained a quantity of Federal American Eagle 62-grain Green Tip. The 62-grain full offers greater penetration than the original 55-grain FMJ load, and excellent accuracy at longer range. The rifle gets better the more it is fired, and in short order had digested 150 rounds of this loading. Since I was using iron sights, the shooter was an important part of the equation, and the Colt features a general-purpose trigger, not a target-grade trigger. It is controllable under all conditions and doesn't limit a skilled shooter, at least at 100 yards. The rifle seems to be capable of 2 MOA or better. The American Eagle loading is well worth the time and effort to obtain and keep in the ready bag in quality magazines.

At a later date the Colt was fitted with a Redfield BattleZone scope and DNZ scope mounts. The rifle was made the designated long range AR-15 in the battery. The Hornady .223 55-grain JSP (Hornady #80256) has proven capable of 1 MOA off the benchrest. The rifle is my favorite AR-15. I have also fitted a LaserMax laser to the forend to maintain in-house combat ability.

Colt M4 Expanse

Colt remains the AR-15 rifle by which all others are judged. There seemed to be a race to the bottom in price and cutting corners. Despite the performance of these rifles, they sell and sell well. Another phenomenon that I find more interesting is the availability of good quality rifles at a fair price. CORE 15 offers their M4 Scout at a fair price, and the rifle is both tight and good. It is supplied without sights. Smith & Wesson has introduced an inexpensive version of their popular Military and Police AR-15 rifle. Smith & Wesson deleted the dust cover and forward assist from this rifle as a cost-cutting measure. Colt's rifles stood at the top of the heap on quality and the cheaper rifles stood on cheap. But with the CORE rifles and the Smith & Wesson there are good quality rifles selling for considerably less than any Colt. These rifles offer a good template for later customization and accessorizing, or are just fine for use as issued. Colt responded with the Colt M4 Expanse. The Expanse

The author mounted a TruGlo scope to the Colt Expanse. This was a great combination.

is delivered without sights, without a forward assist, and without a dust cover. Unlike the Smith & Wesson M&P, however, the Colt may be retrofitted with a dust cover if desired. My first impression is good. The rifle's fit and finish are good, the build quality is excellent, and the carrier keys are properly staked. The bore is chrome lined. The safety, magazine release, and trigger action are all crisp and positive in operation. Attention to detail is evident in the rifle. Trigger compression is 6.5 pounds, the norm for production AR-15 rifles. The trigger breaks clean without creep or backlash. It isn't the

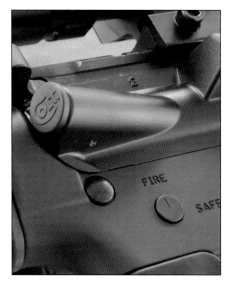

The Colt Expanse does not have a forward assist, but one may be easily fitted if desired.

lightest, but it is reliable and will be familiar to many soldiers and marines who wish to own a good quality AR like the one carried in service. There is no play in the controls. and the rifle feels like any other Colt. The 16.1-inch carbine barrel features a fast 1:7 inch twist. This means the rifle will stabilize the heavier class of bullets, including the 77-grain bullets. Since the rifle came without sights, the next step was to acquire a proper set of optics. There is nothing wrong with iron sights or red dot sights, but I was also interested in fitting a versatile all-around scope to explore the accuracy potential of the rifle. I chose the TruGlo Tactical Illuminated riflescope.

Initial firing was accomplished sighting the rifle in with the TruGlo scope. I carefully lubricated the carrier assembly, did not expect any malfunctions, and did not experience any. For initial range work, I used Hornady #80274 55-grain JHP. This is a steel-cased load offered in a fifty-round box for economy. The rifle is supplied with a single magazine. Additional magazines used included the Brownells magazine, a proven magazine and winner of US military contracts. The rifle was sighted in using the box method. I use the 200-yard zero, with the rifle dead-on for combat ranges, a bit high at 100 yards, and dead-on again at 200 yards. I left the rifle on the 1X setting and proceeded to address a number of modern tactical targets from Tactical

Target Systems. These targets make training interesting and serve a real purpose in tactical training. The TruGlo scope proved to be true to its claim. At moderate ranges, 25–50 yards, the rifle and scope combination proved fast and effective. The trigger is controllable and the rifle is well balanced. When using the preferred hand forward method of firing the rifle, control is excellent. If you are used to the KeyMod rail you may touch the gas block of the standard M4 rifle. This isn't something you wish to do.

Absolutes

I fired one hundred fifty rounds in the initial range testing. It doesn't take long, but I do not like to overheat a barrel, so there was an interval in between the firing strings. I cleaned the barrel and chamber and addressed 100-yard accuracy. I used three loads, the Hornady #8026 60-grain Interlock, the Hornady #80268 75-grain TAP and the aforementioned steel case load. I fired three three-shot groups at a long 100 yards with each cartridge, using the 4X setting. Results were good. The steel case load averaged 1.6 inches, excellent for an economical training load, while the 60-grain JSP averaged 1.25 inches. Interestingly this load averages 0.9 inch in the much more expensive Colt SOCOM. The TAP load is a highly developed load intended for critical use. This load averaged 1.3 inches with a single 1.0-inch group. Clearly, the Colt Expanse is accurate enough for any foreseeable chore. The Colt has proven reliable and clearly accurate enough for any chore short of long-range varmint control. America's first black rifle is still at the top of the heap.

Daniel Defense

One of my friends convinced me to try this rifle. I am glad I did. There are many opportunities to own a great rifle. There are even high-dollar, celebrity-branded rifles that allow you to pay a premium to get the other guy's name on your gun. And then there are the basic claptrap rifles that work most of the time and are okay for plinking. They are a little loose and tie up on occasion, but hey, we are only shooting paper, right? There are better rifles in the upper strata of dead accurate, dead reliable rifles that represent real value for the money. One is Daniel Defense. You can pay more for a rifle, but with the Daniel Defense basic model you'll get something you can count on. A rifle you can count on may not have the same relevance to you and I as it does to the brave young men and women who are going into the sandbox, but then

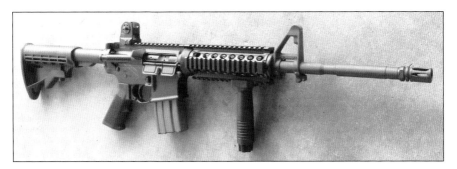

The Daniel Defense rifle has provided excellent protection for many Americans.

I suspect we all would rather have a rifle that works all of the time. My rifle is the carbine with 16-inch barrel and short gas tube. The front sight on this rifle stands alone; on some models the rail forend is long and extends past the sight. There are a number of options to choose from on the Daniel Defense website. Some are much more expensive than my rifle. The fit and finish of the rifle are good. The pins that keep the AR-15 tight and functional are properly fitted, are flush with the receiver, and the stock isn't loose. The finish is even, and the parts mesh together as they should, not as if they were rushed out the door. The rifle's barrel is chrome lined, hammer-forged, with a 1:7 twist. The rifle was supposed to be shipped with a forend grip, but there wasn't one in the box. I purchased this rifle pre-shortage and it had been around the shop a while; it may even have been a used rifle. I bought a different brand forend grip and was good to go.

By the way, in the current shortage and panic buying it seems quite a few folks have purchased a Modern Sporting Rifle and a ton of ammunition. They felt pretty good until the credit card bill came, or Junior needed new running shoes. The guns are then resold at a loss I would call a whipping. Be an astute shopper and you may find a few of these when the panic buying slows down.

Omega Rail

The Omega free-floating rail is a superior forend design that adds to the rifle's versatility and accuracy. The Omega forend cures a number of problems, including the propensity of damage to the bolt that may occur with a conventional forward handgrip. If the barrel isn't free-floating, then pressure on the forward grip may cock the barrel and damage the bolt or chamber during cycle. Don't doubt this one; it comes from the authority, the US Army. The conventional attachment may result in flex on the barrel, and the bolt may strike the chamber off-center, cracking a locking lug. The Omega forend is the superior setup for rigidity, as well as for mounting lasers and lights. No matter what type of gear you choose to mount on the Omega rail, reliability is maintained and point of impact, as related to the point of aim, does not shift. The rifle came with fixed front and rear sights. The Daniel Defense sights are excellent battle sights, capable of delivering good accuracy well past 100 yards. Adjustment of the rear sights are exact and, once set, the sight locks into the indents in a positive manner. The sight does not fold down, but it is removable. I like this one a lot. While many of us will wish to mount an optical sight, the rifle does yeoman service just as issued. The rear sights have the typical large and small apertures for short- and long-range use. The rifle is used for informal practice and instruction. As a certified NRA instructor, I find that even parents who may have little interest in firearms themselves often have children who are interested in firearms. They will then care enough to get training for the child. The Daniel Defense rifle has given quite a few teens their first taste of a center fire Modern Sporting Rifle. Some have gone on to military careers, and the DD M4 gave them a head start on understanding the AR-15 rifle. One of these young men placed at the top of his class at Paris Island! This rifle is accurate. It is a good choice for all-around use.

The CORE 15 Rifle

The Core 15 rifle tested is the basic Scout. The best shot I know recommended this rifle. They begin with Mil-Spec, he says, and make it a little tighter. There is no one whose opinion I respect as much as this able young man. The rifle illustrated is one of several models offered. If you purchase a cheap AR-15, you will have to replace it at some point when you reach the skill level at which the firearm is limiting your performance. With the CORE rifle, you may add a superior optic or front rail at a later date and the platform remains good quality. I like the

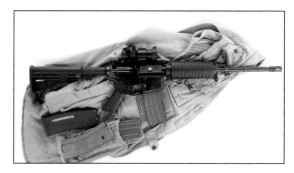

The CORE 15 rifle is among the tightest rifles as issued, and is possibly the best buy in America.

Scout rifle for faster work and will probably leave it as issued. I think that it doesn't make horse sense to start with a cheap rifle. For this test, I began my examination by popping open the receiver and checking the bolt. The bolt carrier key must be properly staked or the rifle simply isn't worth having. The CORE carrier looks good. Next, I checked the trigger. Trigger

This CORE 15 rifle went through a grueling test and never stopped running.

compression is smooth enough, with some take-up and a clean break. The rifle is delivered without sights, so I added a carrier with aperture sights. A good fit and all looked well. The rifle is supplied with a single magazine. I added a stack of PMAGs and various aluminum magazines from Brownells. They have been proofed in months of use, so any problems would have been due to the rifle or ammunition, not the magazines.

A concern: the rifles are packed in grease as delivered. They are shipped all over the country and may sit in a warehouse under conditions CORE cannot control. Strip the packing grease away from the bolt and chamber. Heavily lubricate the rifle for a break-in period; the CORE is that tight. You must do this for proper function. When breaking in a rifle, a good choice of clean burning, but affordable, ammunition is a good place to start. The Black Hills Ammunition 55-grain FMJ loading was used. Accurate, clean-burning, and always reliable, this is a number one resource for checking function in a new AR-15 rifle. I lubricated the rifle well and locked in the first magazine. I load twenty-five rounds in the thirty-round magazines. These first twenty-five rounds were far from boring, but were uneventful. I had a few short cycles that disappeared after the first two magazines. After this modest break-in, every load fed, chambered, fired, and ejected normally. The rifle was sighted in at 25 yards and then 50 yards. Fifty yards is about the limit of my ability to register excellent groups with iron sights, but the 100-yard groups are not bad, just below the potential of the rifle. It is no mean trick to keep three shots in 2 inches at 50 yards with iron sights, which I consider good off the benchrest. I fired a few of the Black Hills Ammunition 60-grain JSP loads, as well. These are excellent service grade loads. I also fired a quantity of the new BHA 77-grain GMX "water resistant" service load. Frankly, with an iron-sighted rifle it is almost just making brass to test such a load at long range, but they each proved more accurate by a margin than the FMJ load. I like to confirm zero with a new rifle, just in case I get that shot at a coyote or broadside a deer. I also fired five rounds of a dwindling supply of the Black Hills Ammunition 52-grain MATCH loading. This is a loading with much to recommend at the 100-yard mark. Settling into a solid firing position off the benchrest, I kept the rifle as solid as possible and squeezed the trigger straight to the rear with concentration on the sights. I took about a minute per shot. I usually fire three shots at 100 yards, but fired five. I managed a five-shot group of just over 2.5 inches using the smaller aperture. Perhaps I will scope the rifle at a later date. It is accurate enough, but then it is a fast-handling problem solver at shorter range. This is my second CORE rifle, and the earlier version performs in a similar manner. The test rifle has been fired with a number of factory loads, and also my personal hand loads. The rifle has proven accurate, reliable, and fast handling. The break-in malfunctions have not repeated themselves. After several months, the grand total is perhaps 1,600 rounds. All brass cased. I chose not to abuse my rifle with steel-cased ammunition. Good performance. This rifle has earned a place in my battery.

Smith & Wesson M&P Sport

This rifle is a value line version of the Smith & Wesson Military and Police AR-15 rifle. I purchased it new for less than seven hundred dollars. This is the rarest of items—an affordable AR-15 rifle with excellent reliability and over-all performance. While an entry level rifle, the Sport version features quality

The Smith & Wesson M&P Sport is a best buy with good performance.

lockwork. The package is basic: a black rifle with a single Magpul thirty-round magazine. There is no quad rail, but a modified GI-style handguard. If you wish, the flattop receiver offers a place to park an optical sight. The rails are marked for easy repeatability if you remove and wish to remount the sight. If you look further, you find a rifle with a properly staked carrier key riding with the bolt assembly. The rifle does not have a forward assist lever nor dust cover. With modern loads, the forward assist may be redundant; there is little that cannot be done by racking the bolt with the cocking handle. The barrel is of good steel and is coated with Melonite. I have used several Smith & Wesson pistols with this covering and have no complaints. Both the bolt carrier and carrier key mentioned earlier are chrome plated. The barrel is stamped 1:9 rate of twist. The rear sight is a modern aperture that folds down and pops back up with ease. The front sight is the standard AR-15 adjustable post. The forward handguard is an improvement on the GI type. It works fine for most shooting styles. I found that the stock does not limit challenging firing sessions and hitting the target quickly. The rear stock is the modern AR-15 adjustable type. It works as well as any other. This is no base rifle and it is not primitive grade. It is simply a quality rifle with fewer features. I have a tenacious memory for test subjects, and the rifle performed as well as any in the reliability department. I react to a badly performing rifle in the same manner I react to a bad odor: I turn up my nose and avoid it. The M&P 15 Sport is a good performer with durable furniture. I am familiar with the type and so were those who fired the rifle, so there was no profane fumbling. This rifle is a good example of a firearm that will protect your home and keep you from the attention of the Grim Reaper. I began the test fire by adding a number of Magpul magazines to the single unit supplied. The initial magazines were loaded with HPR 55-grain FMJ loads. I finished off partial boxes of mixed loads from several makers without a glitch. I locked the bolt to the rear, inserted a loaded magazine, dropped the bolt, and began the test program. The rifle continued to fire well over three hundred rounds without a single failure. The trigger is smooth and crisp, typical of factory trigger actions at about six pounds. The rifle handled well in short-range high-speed drills. The combination of a combat-size rear aperture and post front sight resulted in good hits from 25–50 yards on demand. The day was clear, but a high wind had sprung up. Just the same, the rifle never failed to connect when the sight picture was valid and the trigger properly stroked. It doesn't take long for a group of interested shooters to create a pile of brass with the AR-15 rifle. The rifle is light on the shoulder and pleasant to fire. This is America's rifle, and the black rifle is associated with home and family, as well as with many pleasant range trips. This Smith &

The author fitted a Blue Force sling and Burris red dot to his SW rifle with good results.

Wesson will do the business. I have fitted a Burris Fast Fire 3 Red Dot, and the rifle is at the top of the go-to list.

Ruger AR-556

Ruger's initial offering of a piston-operated AR rifle, the SR-556, is a good rifle, but an expensive one. It is also heavier than the standard AR-15. Ruger decided to offer a standard AR-15 type rifle in the entry level price range. Here is a tip: the AR-556 is as reliable and rugged an AR-15 rifle as you will ever hold. It is easily upgraded with parts, stocks, and optics if necessary, but as issued this is an effective and accurate rifle. It is chambered in 5.56mm and weighs a standard 6.5 pounds. Ruger has kept the price reasonable by employing an intelligent manufacturing process, and has managed to make life easier for AR-15 shooters along the way. The receiver is aluminum and the rifle is a flattop design. It is supplied with a folding polymer rear sight and A2-type fixed-front sight. The 16-inch barrel features a 1:8 rate of twist. This twist is ideal for most uses and has provided good results with a variety of loads in 40- to 77-grain weight. Ruger's barrel isn't chrome lined. A good touch is that the rear face of the front sight is serrated. Ruger also modified the AR-15 handguard arrangement. The handguard is the standard M4 type with internal heat shield. In contrast to the usual spring-loaded ring to secure the handguard, Ruger uses a polymer ring that makes changing the handguard much easier. The controls are all typical AR-15 layout; don't mess with success. The rifle retains the dust cover and forward assist. The six-position shoulder stock is a standard AR-15 type. The firing handle is comfortable to hold, with serrations for adhesion when firing. The trigger action is good, breaking at 6.5 pounds. The gas key is properly staked and the gas key opening is chromed. The bolt carrier's interior is also chromed. The rifle has surprised me with not good, but excellent performance. In the initial range testing I found the standard sights were perfectly sighted for the 100-yard range, with no need for adjustment. A lot of firing was done with the Black Hills Ammunition 55-grain FMJ "Blue Box" load and Brownells magazines. What has followed has been excellent service. The rifle has been fired more than most based upon this performance, and to gauge the result with a variety of ammunition. I determined that the Ruger AR-556 is a great truck gun and home defense gun. I admit I would have preferred a chrome-lined bore but the rifle always works and it is more accurate than I expected. Using iron sights at 50 yards, two-inch three-shot groups with the Black Hills Ammunition Blue Box 55-grain FMJ was easily obtained. However, I spent one evening with the TruGlo scope mounted in order to gauge the rifle's accuracy at a long 100 yards. I used my own handloads using the Sierra 69-grain bullet, Black Hills Ammunition 77-grain Tipped Match King, and the Nosler 64-grain Personal Defense load. Most of the loads broke 1.5 inches, with the Nosler exhibiting a 1.4-inch average. This is a rifle well worth its price.

The Leupold scope and Ruger rifle were a good fit.

These are just a few of the many AR-15 rifles available. The bottom line is this: let these rifles be a comparison to any other rifle considered. A rifle less expensive than the CORE 15 may be a product on which corners were cut in the wrong places. The Battle Rifle Company isn't as well-known as Colt, but performance was at least comparable. Daniel Defense is a good choice. The Smith & Wesson offers a good buy from a major maker. The Ruger may be the best bet for the money. Look closely, keep your guard up, and choose wisely.

Ruger's AR-556 is an excellent all-around patrol and defense rifle.

CHAPTER FIVE

PISTOL-CALIBER CARBINES

When the subject of long arms for police and armed civilians comes up, we are all in agreement. A long gun is better than a handgun. But when the caliber is discussed we sometimes provoke an argument. There are many who find the pistol-caliber carbine suitable for critical use, who feel that the increased accuracy of the pistol-caliber carbine is a great advantage over the handgun, and who believe that increased accuracy potential is all that is needed. Adherents of the pistol-caliber carbine point out that modern calibers, such as the .45 ACP +P, are more powerful than the .44-40 WCF that was a stable of lawmen during the days of the old west. The .40 Smith & Wesson is comparable to the .38-40 WCF.

It's important to note that the old Winchester DASH cartridges were originally rifle cartridges that were adapted to revolvers. Later efforts were concentrated upon rifle cartridges for cops and soldiers. While shorter and

A pistol-caliber carbine can be a joy to use and fire.

less powerful than the .30-06 Springfield, the .351 WSL and the .30 US Carbine rifle cartridges were successful developments. But that is history, and today we need to know exactly what we are getting into with a pistol-caliber carbine. I use the old guns for reference because the level of power they had was used to kill deer, bear, and men. The first thing we have to consider today is the mission and, next, tool selection. If the mission is basically urban or home defense, the pistol-caliber carbine is viable.

There are two basic types of pistol-caliber carbines: lever-action and self-loading. Do not dismiss the lever-action rifle out of hand. The cowboy action assault rifle, as it is sometimes called, has much to recommend it as an all-around, go anywhere, do anything rifle. The self-loaders include the Auto-Ordnance Thompson, UZI, and a few others that are based upon submachine guns. The difference is that the civilian legal versions have longer (legal) barrels than the military SMG, and they are capable of semiautomatic fire only. Other carbines, such as the Beretta Storm and the High Point, are purpose-designed carbines developed independently of any military design. Semiautomatic SMGs may be a contradiction in terms, but that is what we have in the case of the Thompson and the UZI. Rather than the military open bolt, these carbines fire from a closed bolt. The lever-action rifles chambering the pistol cartridges are primarily based upon the Winchester 92 lever action, a rifle praised for its leverage and fast action. The SMG-based carbines are large and heavy. But they are among the most proven carbines, as they are based upon military designs. Thirty-round magazines are readily available. When it comes to accuracy and power, SMG types do not look very good compared to the relatively light and compact AR-15 type rifle. The AR-15 is highly developed and reliable, given a quality version. The purpose designed pistol-caliber carbines are lighter than the SMG-based designs. They are also less proven and are often limited in magazine capacity. When you consider period literature and after-action reports of men issued the SMG in wartime, a common thread seems to be "keep the selector switch on semi-auto." Conversely, another author who did not trust the 9mm for pistol use noted that

With thirty rounds of pistol ammunition on tap, the carbine has some merit.

the effect of several bullets striking at once from an SMG was a different story and very effective. Civilian models have no selector switch, and qualified "officers" with the automatic capacity may be best served by keeping the switch on semi, as well, for most uses. The first look in comparison to the .223 rifle seems to overwhelmingly favor the rifle-caliber carbine.

The Thureon Defense carbine has proven to be accurate and reliable.

There are other considerations. Most domestic gun battles take place within 50 yards. Twenty-five yards is a long range for most defensive situations. The carbine isn't about increasing range, but about increasing accuracy and wound potential. The carbine may be used to dust predators off the homestead, but that is a secondary consideration. Shooters often deploy the pistol-caliber carbine as a home defense firearm. They do not trust their skill with a handgun, or they cannot tolerate the recoil of a shotgun. I think that

The Kel-Tec carbine is neat and handy, and is more accurate than any handgun.

This bolt handle reciprocates as the Kel-Tec carbine is fired.

Just fold up the Kel-Tec for storage.

even the most skilled handgun shooter is wise to adopt a long gun when possible. The pistol-caliber carbine is a pleasant recreational shooter, while the shotgun is not a joy for most of us. The pistol-caliber carbine's muzzle report is less offensive than the rifle when fired indoors. Depending upon the model, the pistol-caliber carbine is less expensive than a rifle caliber carbine. If you choose a High Point or Kel-Tec carbine, the carbine costs less than most quality handguns.

An issue worth our discussion is commonality of magazines. As an example, you can deploy a Glock 17 9mm handgun and purchase a Kel-Tec carbine that uses the same magazines. This is convenient but not a tactical necessity. Operators on the front line deploy the .223/9mm or .308/.45 combination. I think that it is more important to have commonality between the handguns used by a team, or even by a couple who own but two hand-guns. In short, if you cannot hit with the carbine you will not hit with a pistol, and a lot of rounds simply aren't going to be expended in most personal defense situations. You will not run dry of rifle magazines and dig on the pistol belt for spares. Many pistol-caliber carbines, such as the High Point and the Thompson, use a purpose-designed magazine that is not compatible with any pistol magazine. Then there is the person who owns a carbine but not a pistol. In some jurisdictions, the handgun is more difficult to obtain and legally deploy. This is especially true when traveling. The pistol-caliber carbine makes a fine "Brooklyn Special." To be viable the pistol-caliber carbine must stand on its own merits, rather than as an adjutant to the pistol.

Lever-action rifles in pistol calibers served an important purpose in the Old West. When you were far from resupply, the carrying of two firearms

The High Point carbine is not at the top of our wish list, but the example tested was reliable and more accurate than most handguns.

chambered for the same cartridge made sense. The .44-40 WCF was a sterling cartridge by the standards of the day, far more useful than the previous .44 Henry. But even then there were compromises. The .44-40 WCF was a better carbine cartridge than the .45 Colt. The .44-40 featured higher velocity and shot flatter than the .45 Colt, and does so today compared to the .45 Colt lever-action carbine. (The .45 Colt is a relatively recent addition to the lever-action family.) The .44-40 features a bullet with greater penetration and sectional density than standard .45 caliber bullets. On the other hand, the original .45 Colt loading hit harder at close range from the handgun. In short, the .44-40 was the better rifle cartridge and the .45 the better handgun cartridge. There was some compromise in the adoption of a .44-40 handgun and rifle combination. Once lawmen had the .30-30 rifle, most adopted this rifle for its obvious advantages. Today there are lever-action rifles chambered for the .357 Magnum and .44 Magnum, among other calibers, up to and including the .454 Casull. These rifles should be chosen on their own merits, not necessarily tied to the handgun choice. The lever-action rifle is a low maintenance item with a reasonable reserve of ammunition. Many are accurate to 100 yards. Unlike the self-loader, the lever gun may be topped off one round at a time and may be fired with relatively light loadings. Of all the widely distributed pistol-caliber carbines, the .357 and .44 Magnum have the most impressive wound ballistics and seem the most practical.

A general consensus exists that carbines are stronger than handguns and may digest more powerful loadings within the same caliber. This led to the introduction of rifle-only loads in the Winchester DASH calibers, including the .32-30 and the .44-40. In 9mm there were SMG-only loads. We were taking the chance of wrecking one firearm, the pistol, in order to increase the

The Thureon Defense .45 carbine was easily the most accurate and reliable pistol-caliber carbine tested.

power and range of another, the SMG or carbine. My experience does not necessarily reflect an advantage in the carbine in taking heavy loads. In fact, the opposite is true. When working with the blowback action Marlin Camp carbine in both 9mm and .45, I noted that these self-loaders were less reliable with +P ammunition.

The Thureon Defense handguard is well designed.

The carbines never seemed to jam with standard pressure ammunition, but the .45 in particular began to short cycle when fed +P ammunition. Blowback-operated carbines will never be as reliable as gas-operated full power rifles. Those that are, such as the Thompson and UZI models, require a very strong recoil spring that may be difficult for some shooters to properly actuate when racking the bolt. My experience with the .44 Magnum carbine does not reflect greater strength in the action. Two decades ago I was using a pair of .44 Magnum revolvers for hunting. I also owned a Marlin .44 Magnum lever-action rifle. When the Marlin was fired with my standard handload for the handguns (Smith & Wesson 629 and a Ruger Redhawk), the Marlin locked up. I had to apply considerable force to the lever to disengage the action. My handload, using 23.0 grains of a popular powder as stated in the *Speer Reloading Manual* as the max, had to be reduced to 21.5 grains in the Marlin. This load had given no trouble in the revolvers. There are other considerations in using the lever-action rifle, such as trimming cases and different crimping procedure. If you stick to factory loads the problem does not exist, but in my experience the vaunted greater strength of the carbine isn't true, and you are losing some of the advantages of the commonality between the carbine and the pistol by using carbine-only loads.

The handling and accuracy advantage of the pistol-caliber carbine compared to a handgun are obvious. The three-point hold and long sight radius make hitting much easier than with a handgun. Just the same, as far as the bottom line goes, a quality handgun such as the Kimber Gold Combat, Springfield TRP or a Smith & Wesson Mountain Gun, will often produce a 50-yard slow fire group comparable or better than that exhibited by the average shot with a pistol-caliber carbine. The .223 rifle completely outclasses either at 50–100 yards. But power is another question. It is commonly believed that the longer barrel of a carbine increases the velocity of a handgun cartridge by some 300 fps. Sometimes this is true, but a more modest increase is the average, on the order of 150 to 200 fps. This is a significant advantage. A 9mm becomes a .357 SIG, the .40 Smith & Wesson rivals the 10mm, and a .45 ACP becomes a .45 +P, something on

The Storm Carbine proved reliable and uses Beretta pistol magazines.

this order. This increase in power, coupled with the higher hit probability of the carbine and the control inherent in fast repeat shots, make the pistol-caliber carbine far more effective than a handgun on every score. There is no denying this. Just the same, a rifle caliber offers more effect.

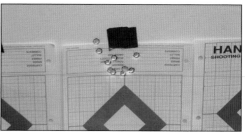

The Beretta carbine is accurate and a good all-around home defense carbine.

The .223 rifle actually provides less offensive ballistics for urban use. If the bullet strikes a body the .223 bullet is more frangible. When striking a hard surface, the .223 high velocity bullet is less likely to ricochet. This has been proven in a number of test programs, but some folks just do not seem to get it. On the other hand, the .223 will penetrate car doors in a superior fashion than the pistol-caliber carbine. Once your mind is made up on a pistol, caliber ammunition selection becomes important. A common misconception exists concerning pistol ammunition when fired from a carbine. I admit I held this misconception, as well. Many of us assumed that, since the carbine exhibited greater velocity with a given load, the bullet may be convinced to expand much more quickly than when the same load was fired in a pistol. The result is less penetration, and perhaps even fragmentation. This conception may have been valid in the days before the Hornady XTP bullet. However, tests showed that the increased velocity from a carbine does result in greater bullet expansion, but also in greater penetration. This was a surprise, although it should not have been. My tests results were obtained using simple water jugs. Since water jugs are six inches wide, it is easy enough to gauge penetration. There is a useful difference in the power exhibited by a pistol-caliber carbine. I have included some of my test results. In the end, I determined that the pistol-caliber carbine is viable in many situations. Convenience, ammunition availability, mild recoil, and low report are important considerations to some of us. Be certain the carbine is reliable with your chosen load. The only reason you might not be well armed is a lack of practice.

The Beretta Storm handles well in close quarters.

NOTES ON PISTOL-CALIBER CARBINES

The SMG types are the least suitable for home defense. The Thompson, as an example, is heavy and doesn't handle quickly. While well made of good material, the Auto-Ordnance Thompson simply isn't a viable home defense firearm, although the deterrent value would be high. This type is usually reliable with quality ammunition. As for

The Beretta is a well-made and reliable carbine with good features.

the UZI, negative connotations and public perception should be considered. Reliability is also an issue. Personally, I have seen several Norinco UZI types at the range and have owned one.

I have never seen an example that could be counted on for reliable function with even one magazine of ball ammunition. The only reliable UZI seems to be the one made in Israel. In other carbines, the Kel-Tec models are

Hornady's TAP loads are excellent performers from the .40 carbine.

light, easily stored by folding, and in my experience they have proven reliable. In testing the 9mm versions I went to several hundred rounds without cleaning. I think that .40 caliber versions are more ammunition sensitive, but with suitable loads are also reliable and hit hard. The Highpoint is a minimal carbine made to sell at a certain price point. Yet the High Point offers an option for a tight budget. The Highpoint usually works. A family member on a strict budget owns a Highpoint .45 as his only firearm. So far it has digested at least three hundred rounds of 230-grain Winchester FMJ without a problem and a few Winchester PDX 230-grain loads. It will not win an accuracy contest, but inside the home it would cut a one-hole group for a magazine of cartridges. The Thureon Defense carbine has given excellent results in testing. It is lighter than the average AR-15 and easy to operate. Accuracy has been satisfying, equaling or exceeding other carbines. Accuracy is at least comparable to the Beretta Storm, and the Thureon takes Glock magazines. The Beretta Storm was developed as an adjutant to Beretta service handguns. The Storm offers excellent handling, good accuracy, and reliable function. If the pistol-caliber carbine is deemed enough for your needs, the Storm is a credible option.

In the below table, you see the results of a comparison between a pistol and a carbine with the same ammunition. For the 9mm ammunition, I used a Beretta 92 and a Kel-Tec carbine. For the .45 ACP comparisons, I used a Colt Government Model 1911 and an Auto-Ordnance Thompson carbine.

	Velocity	Penetration	Expansion
9 mm			
Black Hills 115 gr. exp. (pistol)	1255 fps	9 inches	.64
Black Hills 115 gr. exp. (carbine)	1444 fps	11 inches	.69
Win. Ranger T 124 gr. (pistol)	1198 fps	12 inches	.62
Win. Ranger T 124 gr. (pistol)	1390 fps	14 inches	.69
.45 ACP			
Black Hills 185 gr. JHP (pistol)	1050 fps	13.8 inches	.66
Black Hills 185 gr. JHP (carbine)	1280 fps	15 inches	.72

Is there a useful difference in power? In the author's opinion, a worthwhile advantage. If the arm is used at 50 yards, you are delivering about the same slap as the pistol at conversational range. Keep your head on straight when dealing with pistol-caliber carbine ballistics. As an example, we were required to raise the ladder sight on the Thompson .45 to stay on target at 100 yards. The Thompson is a carbine, but it still fires a pistol cartridge.

CHAPTER SIX

SOMETIMES YOU NEED A .308

The .223 rifle is the go-to choice for modern shooters. Among the advantages is the frangibility of the projectile. The .223 is less offensive in penetration than most handgun rounds. A good loading, such as the Black Hills 60-grain JSP I prefer, will remain in the body in most instances. Ricochet and over-penetration is

The .308 rifle has plenty of power and accuracy for most chores.

limited, although the .223 has good light cover penetration against vehicle doors. Recoil is light and accuracy excellent. The military rifle-based police carbine is very reliable in hard use. However, there are situations in which there is a need for more penetration and more power.

Counter-sniping and roadblock use are legitimate areas in which the .308 Winchester may be deployed. Interestingly the .308 is a better CQB rifle than many imagine. The .308 is touted as a precision rifle. A scoped bolt-action rifle with premium load, such as the Black Hills 168-grain A-Max, will exhibit excellent accuracy. In most police situations inside 100 yards, a semi-automatic rifle is accurate enough. When firing at felons behind plate glass or in vehicles, an instant second shot may be needed. The automatic has an obvious advantage. There are other calibers deemed suitable for use in marksman rifles, including the .270, .30-06, and the .300 Winchester Magnum. But there are none with the versatility of the .308 and the easy availability of the .308 in semiautomatic rifles.

SPRINGFIELD M1A1

Among the best choices is the Springfield M1A1. This rifle is based upon the military M14 rifle. The M1A1 is a highly developed rifle with good features. With proper discipline in avoiding damage to the stick magazine during tactical movement, the M1A1 is a fine choice for heavy use. There are aftermarket maga-zines that are cheap and unre-liable. Buy cheap, buy twice.

A combination of EOTech, B Square, and the M1A1 gave excellent results.

There are certain procedures that should be observed. The rear of the bolt, locking lugs, and the lug that fits into the operating rod must be lubri-cated. The bolt must never be allowed to run forward on a chambered round; only feed the rounds from the magazine. The M1A1 features a floating firing pin that could possibly run forward and fire the weapon if you simply allow the bolt to slam forward on a chambered round. This is called a slam fire. Slam fires occur when a shooter attempts to single load the piece at the range when sighting in. *Do not allow this to occur!* The bolt is designed to feed from the magazine and lose some of its energy in doing so. As issued, the M1A1

features excellent aperture sights, suited for both CQB and accurate fire to 100 yards or more. The rear is the ghost ring type, and the front a protected post. My example features a black synthetic stock. The big story is how the rifle shoots.

I tested the rifle with aperture sights, a red dot, and a good tactical scope. During the largest part of the test

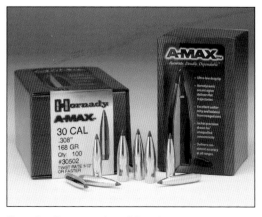

Hornady offers a number of first-class projectiles in .308. The 168-grain A-Max is a favorite.

I used the Black Hills 168-grain BTHP. Quality is excellent and accuracy more than enough for any use. Using the aperture sight, I was able to take a quick bead and get hits on man-sized targets to 100 yards, with rapid follow-up shots. At CQB range I was able to simply look over the front sight and get rapid hits to 25 yards. With attention to the sight picture, head shots typically demanded in hostage rescue operations were no problem well past 25 yards. From a solid barricade, head shots were possible to 50 yards on demand. For use as a patrol rifle or against barricaded felons, it is obvious the Springfield has much merit as issued.

I used an EOTech sight experimentally. This red dot sight is proven in engagements the world over. With a rock-solid B Square mount to secure the EOTech and sight it in for 50 yards, I began the test. Put the dot on the target and you have a hit. At moderate ranges, a combination of a heavy rifle, moderate recoil, and excellent accuracy gave fine results. At this point I qualified a very interesting combination. The Hornady 110-grain TAP load is designed specifically for urban use. With a specially designed bullet jolted to well over 2,900 fps from the Springfield, this is a load guaranteed not to ricochet if hitting a hard object. I have run limited test programs, and I believe this loading would be little more offensive than most .223 loads as far as over-penetration goes, but it would offer superior penetration against sheet metal. This was probably a difficult loading to work up, as bullet pull issues and achieving a full powder burn are no doubt extensive, but the 110-grain TAP loading gave excellent results. Recoil is light, but function in the semiautomatic action good. Several three-shot 50-yard groups included two shots touching. This is a load with much merit. For the destruction of animals or CQB, the loading is a good choice and a credible resource. Many who deploy a .308 rifle will wish to take advantage of long-range accuracy. Accordingly, I took this opportunity to mount a 9×50mm Mueller tactical scope on the M1A1. Complete with Mil-Dot reticule, this is a great scope previously used on the Armalite AR-10 in .300 RSAUM. I sighted the rifle in using the aforementioned Black Hills 168-grain load. For some time, the 168-grain Sierra bullet has reigned supreme due to its high accuracy potential. But it is a hollow point for balance, not for expansion. Since it was originally designed purely as a target bullet, there are times when a non-expanding bullet is less desirable. Wound ballistic could be improved. I qualified the accuracy of this load at 100 yards. I have fired the Black Hills Match load in bolt-action rifles, both sporters and precision rifles. It is not unusual to produce a three-shot group of 0.5 inch or less. (One-half minute or angle or MOA.) A semiautomatic rifle such as the Springfield may produce 2.0 to 2.5 MOA. In this case the rifle gave 2.0 MOA. Even better was the A-Max loading from Black Hills. I was able to fire several groups with this outstanding loading before the barrel heated, affecting the results. I am certain that 1.5 inches on demand is possible, and on one occasion I slipped two bullets into the same hole, with a third opening the group to 1.6 inches. Overall, outstanding results.

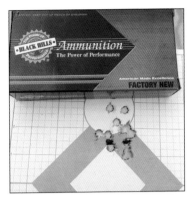

Black Hills Ammunition has proven to be target grade in every rifle.

OTHER .308 RIFLES

The history of the roller cam operated rifle, from the CETME to the HK91, is a thrice-told tale. An epic escape from Nazi Germany by German engineers who took refuge in Spain led to the CETME rifle. The CETME was first adopted in Spain. The CETME served in an era when the M14 and FN FAL were in wide use. The rifle was adopted by a rearming Germany as their G 3. The rifles also became known commercially as the Heckler & Koch HK91. The G3/HK91 has served long and well. The rifle has achieved recognition as both an accurate and reliable firearm. It operates by use of a roller cam mechanism. Rather than using gas operation or a recoiling barrel, the HK91-type rifle operates by use of cams on the bolt that run into a trunnion inside of the receiver. When the rifle fires, the bolt is held steady by the force of the bolt on the roller cams. Once the bullet exits the barrel and pressure subsides, the bolt unlocks and operates in

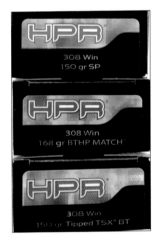

HPR loads have given excellent all-around results in every rifle tested.

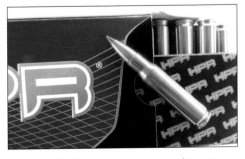

This tipped HPR loading has given good accuracy.

the normal fashion, moving to the rear under spring pressure and then traveling forward to strip a round from the magazine. The spent case has been ejected during the bolt's travel, and the new cartridge is fed into the chamber. This occurs much faster than I am able to describe the action.

The author was impressed with every .308 rifle tested.

With the high price of the original HK91 keeping it out of the hands of many of us, there have been a number of attempts to produce a clone of the HK91. Some of these clones use surplus military parts from nations that once used the HK91. Others are built on modern machinery. The Century International Arms C 91 (or C308) is a combination of surplus and new parts. The C 91 is a 9.5-pound rifle with an 18.5-inch barrel. The C 91 is chambered for the 7.62 NATO or .308 Winchester cartridge. The C 91 uses twenty-round box magazines. The rifle is a good all-around shooter for those of us wishing to

When it comes to finesse and quality, the PTR 91 rifle cannot be beat.

Century's C91/C308 rifle is a good shooter.

obtain and use an HK91-type rifle without paying thousands of dollars to do so. The C 91 has advantages over the earlier but similar CETME rifle. It is assembled from surplus parts. The receiver is welded and may have originally been a fully automatic type, but the selector switch is removed or modified. The rifle's safety is an ergonomically designed lever on the left side of the

The PTR safety lever is ergonomic, and positive in operation.

receiver. The fitting of the bolt, cams, and trigger mechanism seems good. The rifle features HK91-type sights and the same stock configuration.

The CETME was a serviceable rifle. However, the flip-up rear sights, with an open aperture for short-range use and a smaller aperture for long-range use, are not as useful as the HK91-type drum sight. The HK91-type sight uses an open sight for short-range use and smaller apertures for 200-meter to 400-meter use. These are among the best combat sights ever used on a battle rifle, in my opinion. The front sight is a shrouded post. The longer-range settings offer a tight sight picture for precision shooting. To load the rifle, first lock the operating handle to the rear. The operating handle is beside the barrel. The handle is raised and the operating rod moved to the rear. This moves the bolt to the rear and cocks the action. The bolt may be locked to the rear. A loaded magazine is then inserted. The operating rod is released and the bolt travels forward, stripping a cartridge from the magazine and into the chamber. The operating rod does not reciprocate as the rifle is fired. The rifle's safety is placed in the safe position after loading. The bolt does not lock open on the last shot. The synthetic forearm features vents to facilitate barrel cooling. There is a checkered portion of the handguard about 4.25 inches long that offers excellent adhesion when firing. The firing grip features a modest thumb riser that allows excellent handling. This handle fits most hands well. The stock is adequate for most users, with a 14.25-inch length of pull. The magazine well allows rapid magazine changes with practice. The magazine release is positive in operation. Trigger compression is heavy but relatively smooth and consistent. The RCBS registering trigger pull gauge registers 10.5 pounds.

There is little take-up in the trigger action and reset is rapid. In firing quickly at close range, and in firing at man-sized targets to 100 yards, the trigger and fixed sights gave good results. When firing for absolute accuracy off a solid benchrest firing position, the rifle gave credible results. The C 91 is a comfortable rifle to fire and use. It is recommended that the rifle be fired one hundred rounds or so for a break-in. This is a common requirement for roller cam operated rifle actions, including the C 91, the PTR 91, and the HK 91 rifle. However, many will come out of the box running. One of the author's rifles did so, while another required a modest break-in. The second rifle suffered short cycles during the first sixty rounds and then operated normally. Winchester white box USA ball is useful for this break-in. Also, all magazines do not fit, function, and lock properly. Magazines specific to the C 91 are best. The original G 3 featured a paddle release similar to the HK P7M8 handgun. Parts kits that end up as the C 91 feature the push-button release.

The best shot we know found the PTR rifle to be a great shooter.

Among the primary loads used for this test was the Winchester USA 147-grain loading. Accurate enough for most chores, clean burning and reliable, this is a good resource for initial tests of any military grade rifle. I also fired a quantity of Portuguese surplus loads. This ammunition is comparable in quality and accuracy to commercial ammunition. Despite the power of the .308 cartridge, recoil remained manageable. The roller cam action seems to soak up a portion of the recoil of this powerful rifle cartridge. When firing offhand the rifle proved lively, tracking targets quickly and responding to a trained shooter. When firing from the benchrest for absolute accuracy, the 200-meter aperture was used, although we fired at 50 and 100 yards. This was for best accuracy; however, the rifle fired several inches high with this setting. When firing for accuracy at 50 yards, the rifle exhibited excellent accuracy. Firing off the bench with a heavy trigger and iron sights produced average groups of 2 inches. A few, with the Black Hills 175-grain MATCH load, were better. I fired a number of three-shot groups at a long 100 yards, using the Black Hills 175-grain MATCH in this effort. The rifle has good accuracy potential, with a single 2.5 MOA group. Most groups, however, were in the 4-inch range at 100 yards. Quality optics would change the equation.

The military stock is okay as far as it goes; however, I elected to go for improved fit in chasing greater accuracy potential. The PRS2 stock from Magpul Industries (Brownell) allows adjustment of the length of pull from about 15 to 16.25 inches. The cheek piece allows changes up to 1.8 inches vertically and fore and aft adjustment of 0.65 inch. The C91 class of rifle has a forward weight bias, and the heavier than standard Magpul stock results in an excellent feel. After some adjustment and range work, I rate this stock a first-class addition to the C 91. For those wishing to mount optics and use the rifle for precision work, including hunting, the PRS2 is a good option. After using the C 91 for several months I am impressed. The rifle is military grade, heavy duty, the build quality seems good, and the rifle is a link with the great rifles of the past. The C 91 is a good all-around .308 rifle for those preferring the roller cam system.

I don't like to recommend rifles not currently in production. It is a case of "I don't buy my rifles, I have them," but a number of the local sheriff's deputies utilize the .308 caliber CETME. This is a good rifle, and a reasonable choice if you know how to maintain the rifle. With prices climbing at present, it is practically half the price of a good M1A1. It would be difficult to mount a scope on the CETME, so it is a finite resource. The rifle features a rugged rear sight with flipping sights offering settings for two and three hundred meters.

Ruger's 7.62 rifle is becoming popular among demanding shooters.

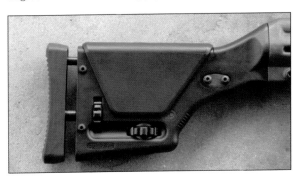

The author fitted this Magpul stock to his Century .308 and enjoyed a great improvement in handling.

The combat sight is an open leaf. The rifle is a joy to fire and use, and certainly makes a good roadblock and patrol rifle for those who prefer the .308. This is an occasional shooter for the author, and the military two-stage trigger takes some getting used to. Just the same, I was able to coax the Black Hills 168-grain BTHP into a 3 MOA group at a long 100 yards, although the average for four groups was 4.5 MOA. My rule is to use this load to work up the rifle before I move to anything else. If the rifle does not feed or group with this Black Hills loading, it is sick. I find the C91 a better rifle, mainly due to the superior sights.

Tips for Using the HK91-Based Rifles

1. Load the magazine.
2. Grasp the cocking handle on top of the barrel.
3. Bring it to the rear and lock the handle in place. That locks the bolt to the rear.
4. Insert a loaded twenty-round magazine.
5. Ensure the magazine locks into place and is seated properly.
6. Release the cocking handle, allowing the bolt to run forward, stripping a cartridge from the magazine and loading it into the chamber. The rifle may be placed on "safe" if you are not going to fire immediately.

It is no surprise that the best of the HK clones is the most expensive. The PTR 91 rifle is a well-made firearm. The sights are proven HK type, with a bold, protected front post. The rear sight is a turret-style battle sight with an open leaf for 100 yards, and aperture rear sight for 200, 300, and 400 yards, with the smaller aperture for longer range. The sight is turned to each setting

The Magpul stock has a wide range of adjustments.

depending on the range. Trigger press is smooth and crisp, but typically heavy at nine pounds. The rifle is comfortable to fire. The push is more than the .223, of course, yet not uncomfortable. The roller-cam action absorbs much of the recoil of the powerful .308 Winchester cartridge. I fired the rifle offhand in fast-moving drills with excellent results to 100 yards. Here is how I do it:

PLACE THE FRONT SIGHT ON THE TARGET.

1. Line up the aperture rear sight.
2. Squeeze the trigger and you have a hit.

This rifle is tighter than the Century clone and demanded a break-in, but once broken in the rifle has continued to provide good function and accuracy. I have fired it with several commercial hunting loads using JSP bullets, and with bullets in the 155- to 168-grain span it functions well. When working up the information in this book I took the PTR 91 to the range, lubricated it well, and settled in with the Winchester 168-grain MATCH load. I fired two magazines, forty rounds, to gauge the accuracy of the rifle. Accuracy testing involved firing three-shot groups at 100 yards. Firing with iron sights for accuracy demands attention to detail, including sight alignment, sight picture, and trigger control. The results reflect the shooter's skill more than the accuracy potential of the rifle. The rifle is worth mounting quality optics, of that I am certain. The average group was 2 MOA; however, on two occasions a three-shot group slipped into 1.5 MOA. The rifle is accurate enough for practical application in the hunting field and as a recreational shooter. More advanced versions than my rifle with optical sights would be better performers. The PTR 91 is well made of good material, and among its most important attributes is that it offers a well-defined pride of ownership.

LOADING THE .308

Handloading is a skill most marksmen realize they must possess. Loading for the semiautomatic requires care in the procedure. I use RCBS small base dies. I was able to work up a load with the Sierra 155-grain Palma that bettered my results with factory loads in most rifles by a margin. Economy loads with the

Although the rifle is larger than the 5.56mm AR, the .308 AR-10 handles in exactly the same fashion.

The best shot we know likes to fire the AR-10 SW M&P.

Sierra 150-grain JSP were quite accurate as well. For practical purposes, the .308 rifle is as heavy and powerful a rifle as we will ever need for defense and sporting use. If you need more power than the .223, the .308 is the name of the game. If you need still more accuracy, the M1A1 may be tuned and tweaked to National Match standards. I think that when we choose a .308 it is for longer range, as when we are hunting deer or other game. If we have a real need for short-range penetration the .308 provides it.

A .308-CALIBER AR: THE AR-10

You gain power, but the question is: do you give up handling with the heavier AR-10? In my opinion, not much at all. The Smith & Wesson Military and Police AR-10 exhibits excellent handling. The flattop receiver accepts any practical optic. The rifle is an AR-15-type with forward assist, standard firing handle, and the same magazine catch and slide lock release we have come to know and love with the AR-15. I replaced the stock with a Mission First Tactical stock from Brownells. This is simply personal custom fitting to the shooter. The receiver, buffer tube, and telescoping stock are familiar to AR-15 shooters around the world. You may modify the rifle as you see fit. I like it as issued, but if long-range shooting is in the cards, you may wish to add good optics and a custom grade forend. Interestingly, this isn't really a copy of the original AR-10, but rather a modified AR-15. The rear of the bolt is AR-15 size, as an example, while the front of the carrier is .308 size. It works out well. There is an improved firing pin spring that may counter slam fires caused by the floating firing pin. Slam fires are most common with poorly-sized handloads or protruding primers. Never place a cartridge in the chamber and then allow the bolt to slam shut. Always load from the magazine. The Smith & Wesson Military and Police 10 has a couple of other advantages over most any other AR-type rifle. The Smith & Wesson features an ambidextrous safety. When training, I do not consider one hand the right hand and the other the left. Rather, I shoot with the rear hand on the handle and the forward hand controlling the rifle. Right- or left-hand operation depends upon the obstacle and the firing position. The barrel isn't a heavy barrel, but it is adequate for the task. The barrel twist rate is 1:10 inches, which proves capable of stabilizing the loads fired with good accuracy. These loads included not only the Winchester USA 147-grain FMJ, but also the Winchester 150-grain JSP and the Winchester 180-grain JSP. Accuracy is good to excellent, with 2–2.5-inch groups at 100 yards with iron sights. The rifle will do better once there are proper optics mounted. There have been no failures to feed, chamber fire or eject with a variety of loads, including handloads. The rifle has proven reliable with bullet weights of 147 to 180 grains, including handloads using the Sierra MatchKing in both 168- and 175-grain weight. The 175-grain bullet is designed to kick the wind better, and to offer good results at ranges well past 200 yards. When firing and handling the rifle, there are several advantages over other short .308 rifles that come to mind. First, the rifle kicks less than most bolt-action rifles. This is because of the gas operated action. The action soaks up and uses recoil energy. Second, the

Winchester offers the affordable USA brand for inexpensive practice, and MATCH loads for accuracy work.

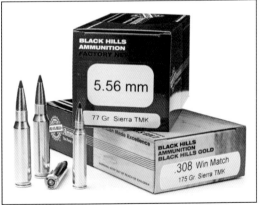

Black Hills Ammunition offers first class loads with outstanding performance.

ergonomics of the rifle are excellent for all-around recoil control. The rifle is reliable. If you need the extra punch of the .308 in the AR-15 platform, this is a great rifle. If you are hunting with a .308 bolt gun and wish to try the AR-15, this is a good place to start. The Smith & Wesson rifle is a good show, with quality, accuracy, and reliability.

If you need superior ballistics and greater barrier penetration, then the .308 rifle is the choice. These self-loaders give you an edge in every regard.

CHAPTER SEVEN

MEDIUM RANGE SHOOTING

O nce you have mastered basic marksmanship and have become a capable shot, you will speed up and also address targets at longer range. The practical ability of being able to connect quickly with an opponent at 50–125 yards is limited only by your practice and determination. Close range combat skills are covered in the next chapter on carbine marksmanship. In this chapter, we are going to cover mid-range marksmanship. There is a big difference in getting reliable hits at 50–125 yards compared to firing at close range, or firing off the benchrest. Some of what we have covered previously will be stressed, as well as considerations for accuracy past the 50-yard mark. This type of shooting is simply an extension of basic rifle skills, and a further integration of these skills. The techniques needed to engage targets at extended range rely upon proficiency with the rifle. This means application of the fundamentals. *No matter how skilled and confident you become, you should practice these fundamentals often.*

This young shooter is carefully practicing the proper shooting stance.

This shooter is holding the rifle into the shoulder, holding the forend, and lining the sights properly.

FIRING POSITION

Whether firing from a standing position or using some type of rest, a good firing position is essential. The kneeling firing position is a great choice for field work if properly applied. Consistency is the watchword. The non-firing hand supports the forend. When firing quickly the hand will be extended toward the end of the rifle stock. When you are in a more secure position and firing more slowly, the hand is sometimes closer to the magazine box. It takes practice to sort this out. A defect in the firing position that I see often is a failure to place the butt of the rifle stock firmly into the shoulder. The rifle butt cannot be allowed to rise on the shoulder. Use the bones of the arm to support the rifle. Let the muscles relax as much as possible. When you have practiced the firing position will be automatic. No matter whether you move from one position to the other, or take cover behind a wall or stand beside a barricade, the rifle will quickly come to the shoulder, the support hand will reach the forend properly, and you will find cheekweld quickly. You must practice assuming different positions without allowing the rifle butt to be levered up and out of the pocket formed by the shoulder. When you are in the firing position you may use cover or concealment. Do not allow the barrel to touch this cover. If the barrel touches cover, or support such as a wall, harmonic vibration will cause the bullet to travel in a different arc. The result is a miss at any range past a few yards. I have tested this extensively. By resting only the handguard on a board or bench, the point of impact will be off by an inch or two at 25 yards; not a great deal, but magnified at longer range. On the other hand, if only the muzzle is rested on the object the barrel recoils away from

The author is practicing quickly bringing the rifle to bear in offhand firing.

This shooter is practicing firing from a braced position.

the rest. The miss may be several inches at 25 yards. So use the hand to rest on the stabilizing object, or at least on the rifle handguard.

Kneeling

I think that kneeling and firing is the most underutilized of the firing positions. It is a stable position that makes for a smaller target area. This position is recommended in the home to give the user stability, and to fire from around cover. The position is high enough to fire over or around cover. The rifle should be grasped in a steady hold with the body slanted at 45 degrees toward the target. The right knee, or firing side knee, is on the ground. Set on the right heel and have the heel in a straight line under the spine. The spinal column offers excellent support.

PRONE

The prone firing position is the steadiest. It is also the slowest to move into and out of, but with practice it can be accomplished readily. To assume the prone firing position, I look toward the target and move into the firing position with the rifle muzzle raised to prevent digging it into the dirt. I then move toward prone, with the rifle extended. If there is a natural support for the forend I use it; otherwise, I use the non-firing hand. The sling may be used to help keep the rifle steady. By keeping the body aligned with the rifle, rather than at an angle, you are able to present as slim a profile as possible,

Excellent work may be done from the braced firing position.

Firing while kneeling affords an ideal braced position in the field when no other option is available.

This shooter is learning to quickly assume the kneeling position.

minimizing the chances of incoming fire striking your body. Recoil is also managed in a superior manner. You should get the heels flat on the ground. This takes practice but should become a natural movement. The heels simply cannot be allowed to provide a target indicator for the adversary. The proper way to assume the prone firing position is to go to the knees, and then to the ground on the non-firing side shoulder, placing the rifle butt strong into the firing side shoulder, and then rolling to prone. Attempting to get the rifle situated after rolling prone is less satisfactory.

Standing

If you must fire at longer range from standing, you need to find some type of support. A tree is good for open country, a wall or pole for urban use. The non-firing hand forms a V and cups the forend with this hand, offering good support.

Never allow the barrel or forend to directly contact the support. A vehicle or pole is good support in the urban tangle. For best stability, the non-firing arm is extended as far as possible. The body is angled 45 degrees toward the target.

This young shooter is learning to quickly assume the prone firing position.

To quickly assume the prone firing position, the shooter first rolls onto his shoulder and presses the rifle into the shoulder.

The rifle is pressed into the shoulder before rolling to the full prone firing position.

Prone fire can be accurate with proper practice.

When using the braced firing position there is a technique that works well: Place the support arm fully extended against the stabilizing wall, pole, tree, or vehicle, and then drop the firing leg slightly to place weight against the support arm. In this manner, you are making the body a solid rest. Using techniques such as this will enable you to eventually become a great marksman.

Shooting Off a Pack or Rucksack

If you have a good backpack, the pack may become a rifle rest. The backpack becomes the greatest multiplier of accuracy: a solid rest. In a hunting situation, this is a good rest. The pack should have a good, solid internal bracing structure. You should choose this type for outdoor use; they are much sturdier than the unsupported type.

The backpack or shooting bag makes an excellent rest to increase accuracy.

If the bracing is external, the rifle may vibrate off the frame. Always keep the support hand between the rifle and the backpack frame. The pack may be placed upright if you are trying a kneeling shot, or if you are going prone the pack may be on the flatter side. I find that bracing the trigger guard or rifle

This shooting bag is reinforced and allows excellent braced fire in the field.

handle on the pack, and supporting the rifle with the hand further out, works well. The trigger guard is usually the balance point of the rifle. Get the rifle in solid on the pack at this point, and then use the support hand to control muzzle angle and elevation.

Bipods

Bipods are a great aid to enable accurate fire at any range. But always remember that *if a rifle is in contact with a hard object the rifle will recoil away from this object.* The bipod is part of the rifle. The bipod doesn't isolate the rifle from a hard surface. The best means of using the bipod is to keep the bipod as close as possible to the ground or support. Let flex be at the minimum. Lean into the rifle with pressure on the bipod. If possible, use the rifle on the dirt

The Champion bipod is a good addition to any rifle.

The rifle bipod is a good multiplier for accuracy (Colt Defense.)

or grass instead of a hard rocky surface. When either the rucksack or bipod are used, the shooter must have confirmed the zero. The rifle will not shoot to the same exact point of aim when braced with the rucksack or the bipod, so confirm the zero at the range using these accuracy-enhancing devices.

AIM

Whatever the shooter's position, the integration of skill begins with aiming the rifle properly. The rifle is pointed toward the target. The rifle is moved to the firing position, the muscles relax in the braced position, and the trigger is pressed. Press straight to the rear, and do not move the sights as the trigger is pressed. Considerations include getting the proper eye relief with the rifle scope. This is the distance from the eye to the rifle scope. The eye relief must be a constant; you cannot allow your focus to waver. From one firing position to the other, there should be as little vari-ance as possible. The eye must face the scope properly. If the neck is stressed, blood flow is restricted and your vision will blur. The rifle scope is brought to the eye, not the eye to the scope, for the best comfort and sight picture. Learning the proper sight picture will give you a supe-rior field of view. When using a scope, the reticle is placed on the center of the target, while an iron front post is usually placed

While center of mass is the ideal shot, we take what we can get when involved in a critical incident.

just below the target. When you perform all the various functions perfectly—hold, trigger press, and sight alignment—then you will get a hit. If there is an error, you will miss. The degree of the error determines the extent of the miss. With the 8-inch kill zone of a deer, the error can be slight and you will still get your buck, but this isn't what we strive for. We strive for a center hit exactly where the sights are pointed, and we strive for this hit every time.

At certain ranges, you will notice an angular displacement of shots. You may miss the bull by an inch at 50 yards. This may be 2 inches at 100 yards. Range magnifies the miss. When you have aimed carefully for the center of the target consistent misses are less frequent, but a miss is a miss whatever the displacement. In sport shooting and hunting this is less important than personal defense. Predator hunting, and protecting the herd and the livestock, often demands precise shooting as the predator is small and you do not wish to miss. In personal defense, public defense, and area defense, the demands are different. If you miss, it could mean you are sitting shiva for a loved one—or they for you. This is the time when you will wish you had bought the best gun for its merits, not the best gun for the money. When engaged in personal defense the aiming point is the center of mass, always. The center of mass is misunderstood. *The center of mass is the center of the target you see.* An adversary will seldom present a full broadside shot. That target will likely not be perfectly squared to you. You may be better trained; the adversary may have an instinct for cover. The center of mass is the center of the exposed target. If the exposed target is just a knee as he fires at you from behind cover, you still take the shot. The target is the center of the exposed mass, in this case a knee. If the body is exposed, the center of mass is near the arterial region of the heart. If only the upper portion of the body is exposed, then the center of mass is a little lower. If the body is bladed toward you, then the center of mass is the center of the thickest point that is in your sights.

The majority of shooting errors occur because the rifle is not properly braced. With proper bracing the rifle will not move as the shot is fired. A jerk of the trigger, rather than the desired press, is also the culprit in a missed shot. Improper sight alignment is another cause of a miss. Another problem that is common with rifles, even the relatively light kicking .223, is flinch. I think that muzzle blast contributes as much to the problem as actual recoil. Flinch is an involuntary muscle reaction that anticipates recoil. The body reacts before the shot is even fired. A rough analogy is the constriction of one's muscles before the injection of a hypodermic needle. We know that relaxing the muscles results in less pain, but it is difficult to do. The same goes for rifle shooting. Flinch destroys accuracy. A good way to combat flinch is constant dry-fire practice. Next, have a range partner hand you your rifle in alternating loaded and unloaded states. If you have flinch you will jerk when the striker falls on an empty chamber. Flinch and jerking the trigger are among the single greatest impediments to accuracy. Flinch may even affect the eyes; you may involuntarily blink just before firing, losing the sight picture.

Follow-through is simply the act of maintaining the sight picture, sight alignment, and grip as the rifle fires. You do not release your hold on the rifle. As the rifle fires, recoil could cause misalignment and a miss if the rifle is not held properly. You must avoid allowing a reaction to muzzle blast and recoil to cause the rifle's sights to move off the target. It is important that you continue to press the trigger, allowing the finger to release the trigger *only after* recoil energy is dissipated. This follow-through doesn't mean you will not lose the sight picture during recoil. You will, but you will be able to quickly reacquire the sight picture.

CHAPTER EIGHT

CARBINE MARKSMANSHIP

FAST AND ACCURATE SHOOTING AT SHORT RANGES

Old West marshals and lawmen kept a Winchester 92 handy for serious use. The handgun was for use in town and the unexpected. Later, the Winchester .351 SLR and the Remington Model 8 were popular. Today carbines are back in the saddle again. Critical events have made the patrol carbine a desirable complement to the peace officer's pistol and shotgun. The complacent

The author finds the Winchester .351 rifle a formidable firearm. Carbine marksmanship has been important for well over one hundred years.

era in which police officers patrolled with only a pistol started to come to an end in the fire and smoke of such infamous incidents as North Hollywood, and more recently San Bernardino. By the same token, homeowners fearing invasions by gangs and takeover robberies have widely adopted the carbine. It may be a pistol-caliber carbine or an AR-15 rifle, but it will be more effective than a handgun. Many agencies, and even private security, started adding rifles or pistol-caliber carbines to their lists of approved tools following the 9/11 attacks. After all, it's likely that if terrorists engage in a firefight with American police officers they will be well armed, possibly outfitted with body armor, and capable of firing accurately at more than 100 yards. A pistol would be next to useless in such a long-range fight against armored subjects. So would most pistol-caliber carbines.

Quickly handling a rifle in the home could be a lifesaver.

The Lasermax green laser is a great addition to the rifle for use in close quarters.

Some say that the need for a rifle is overstated. It is true that it will likely not be needed often. But here's the counter to that argument: When you need a rifle, you need it badly. And the public could be endangered because you don't have one. A well-chosen rifle can be useful from conversational range to several hundred yards. Still, the key factor in successful operation of this weapon is the skill of the operator. When patrol rifles are introduced in many police agencies, they are too often assigned to officers after only minimal training. Many traditional police courses do not adequately address the problems the carbine was introduced to solve. There are many schools of thought about implementing the carbine, but the fact remains that the basics of marksmanship must be mastered before the carbine can be used well. Once these basics are mastered, a good shot can use this tool to keep the peace and resolve incidents involving deadly threat. Too many of us will buy a quality rifle and then not properly maintain it or learn to use it. That is a waste of a good piece of safety gear. There isn't anything mysterious about the carbine. If held properly, the trigger pressed properly, the sights are aligned, and follow-through is respected, the shooter will hit the target. Proper training and practice will limit misses. Practice must include more than basic marksmanship practice in which you shoot at stationary targets from defined ranges. Training scenarios should include: instruction on how to shoot at felons at close range, how to counter multiple threats, how to neutralize threats behind cover, how to target and hit partially exposed threats, how to stop threats in vehicles, and how to eliminate threats at long range. It isn't about shooting, it is about fighting. You will have to take the weapon to the

Maggie Reese of Colt shows how to properly get the grip forward on a Colt AR-15.

range and work it, shooting at different distances, at both stationary targets and moving targets, and using cover when possible.

I use long-range shooting to develop accurate shot placement. I realize these shots will not often be needed, but use them as a training aid. Marksmanship is important, but so is cover and safety. If *you* do not get shot, you have won the game! Your life depends on you remembering that just because you have a rifle you are not impervious to small arms fire. The basics of sight picture, sight alignment, and trigger press should be mastered before you move to effective defensive training. An NRA course is a great idea. You should also understand how to maintain the firearm and keep it lubricated.

Malfunction drills must be practiced. You should begin with a triple check unloaded rifle and practice gripping the rifle, practice moving with the rifle, and become comfortable getting into different firing positions. There are a number of basic shooting positions that you should master in order to be effective with a carbine in a fight. Standing, kneeling, and prone must be thoroughly understood, as should firing around corners and firing from cover.

Firing quickly from kneeling is an important skill.

At the range you are relaxed. Add some stress! Never forget that you are training to act quickly and decisively to save your life or the life of an innocent person. You are not just plinking at targets, and if you think you are then you're in the wrong business. Your time training with your carbine should be all about learning to fight and win. That means you need to practice quick and accurate fire.

SIGHTS

One of the most overlooked skills when using long guns is quickly getting the gun into firing position and acquiring the sights. Without these important skills, all else fails when a quick shot is needed. Most patrol carbines have standard aperture sights. Some of us use red dot sights and others use more powerful long-range optics. Each of these different sights requires different techniques for sight acquisition and alignment. Let's look at the requirements for quickly hitting with different types of sights.

Aperture Sights

When you need to aim quickly using aperture sights—and this applies to a shotgun with ghost ring sights as well—the rear sight should come to your eye first. Your cheek should be welded to the stock at the same time, even for shots at moderate range. The front sight is then pulled into the aperture. It will center itself for an accurate shot. That is the advantage of the aperture: Your eye natu-

Speed is the greatest asset of the red dot sight. Bringing the sight to the eye should be practiced often.

rally centers a post in the rear circle, aperture, or ghost ring. With a little practice, you can easily use an aperture sight on a carbine to make a very fast, very accurate first shot.

Open Sights

With the traditional open sight often found on sporting rifles and on "buck special" or "riot" shotguns, or an AK-47, find the front sight first and then pull the front sight into the rear sight notch. Open sights are not as good as aperture sights for quick action, but with some practice a skilled shooter can make them work.

Even a scope-mounted rifle may be brought to bear quickly at close range with proper practice.

Optical Sights

Any agency or individual officer thinking of fitting a patrol carbine with optical sights should step back for a second and weigh the pros and cons of these devices. A modern rifle scope has many benefits, but contrary to popular belief will not automatically make you a better shot. We have a great love for gadgets, and the optical sight is a great gadget. Some, such as the Nikon M-223, are pretty rugged. However, optics have drawbacks. The scope may be damaged in the trunk of a cruiser. You don't want to get into a fight with an inoperable scope. Finally, shooting well with a scope requires a lot of practice. Be certain that you want to put in that time. There are many advantages to an optical sight. In addition to the magnification that it provides, an optical sight is on a single plane, meaning there is no front and rear sight, only the sight reticule. As a result, it is much easier to focus on the target.

This shooter is practicing firing from cover. This is an excellent firing position.

MAGNIFICATION

While we're at it, let's discuss magnification for a moment. Remember, a patrol carbine is not intended for the same kind of duty as a sniper rifle. That's why, as general issue for police carbines and for personal defense for the rest of us, I suggest an optical sight with the lowest magnification, from no magnification to perhaps four power. Field of view is an issue, especially when you consider that you may have to use your rifle at anywhere from point-blank range to more than 100 yards. The proven method of getting into action with an optical sight is to shoulder the weapon rapidly and take a coarse sight picture over the top adjustment knob of the sight. Lining up on the target with this knob, you then quickly

The Troy Battle Sight draws the eye to the center of the aperture, and the eye then centers upon the front post.

move the eye to the center of the scope. With practice, you will find that this drill may be executed rapidly. An accomplished shooter with much practice may jump directly to the reticle, but for most of us the coarse sight picture drill works well.

The Red Dot (Mueller) is useful even in dim light; the user may keep both eyes open when firing.

Holographic Sights

Holographic dot-type sights, such as those produced by Burris and Mueller, require the shooter to learn new skills. When using one of these sights, shoulder the carbine quickly and find the little red dot in the scope. When the firearm is at the ready, focus on the threat. Keep both eyes open and a red dot will appear. When the red dot is superimposed over the target you will fire. Those used to a standard rifle scope and closing one eye will find learning to shoot with both eyes open difficult, but the advantage is worth the effort.

The author practices quickly bringing the scope to his eye.

Firing braced or from a barricade is an important multiplier of accuracy.

MARKSMANSHIP AND TACTICS GO HAND IN HAND

When using a carbine, maximize the advantages you have. Always take cover and dominate the situation, if possible. If you are firing from cover, with a braced position, you are not only safer from incoming fire but you are far more accurate. You present a smaller target for the bad guys (unless they have the high ground) and also gain the bracing of the earth when you shoot from the prone position. Know how and when to use this skill. Firing prone gives you much steadier aim. However, it also presents you with one key difficulty: you can't change positions as quickly as you can while standing, kneeling, or sitting. And remember, prone behind cover is great, unless the bad guys have an elevation advantage. In that case, if you are stretched out prone, then you are presenting them with a big target. In all firing positions with the AR-15 rifle, maintain control by keeping the support hand forward.

Practicing firing at moderate range, quickly, is a good skill building exercise.

When moving and preparing to shoulder the rifle, proper use of the sling is important.

There will be situations when the bad guy is close and you do not have cover. When this happens, there is some danger that the threat might be able to grapple with the long gun. However, by keeping your weapon below eye level you will be able to see him or her make this move and react to it. Am I advocating that you train to use a carbine at extreme close range without even bothering to aim? No. Our carbine has much better balance and natural point than a handgun and, at three to ten feet, firing below eye level can work. With the three-point attachment of the long gun, accuracy in quick unaimed fire is much better than that of a handgun. Point with the front sight, and remember that the bullet will impact high if placed on the navel if you use only the front sight.

The carbine is a great multiplier of marksmanship. Solid hits can be made at great range, and rescue shots are possible with the carbine that would never be possible with a handgun. But with this advantage comes the responsibility of mastering the firearm.

Even if you are involved in a home defense situation, the sling can be important. The Blackhawk! Tactical Sling is a smart addition to the rifle.

CHAPTER NINE

QUICKLY GETTING THE RIFLE INTO ACTION

For home or area defense situations, you have made a wise decision if you have chosen a long gun. A rifle gives you a fighting chance in the worst situations. Whatever rifle you choose, you must learn to use it to your best advantage. This means learning to clean, lubricate, and

The author finds that the lever-action rifle is plenty fast and reliable for most uses.

maintain the rifle. This also means learning how to quickly load and unload the rifle and to quickly get it into operation. Let's look at a few of the popular types and their manuals of arms.

LEVER-ACTION RIFLES

Lever-action rifles use a lever under the receiver to move the bolt. Get the fingers into the bolt, not grasping it from below. The bolt is pressed forward, not down, for fast operation. Most lever-action rifles are loaded by a loading gate in the side of the receiver. The cartridges are firmly pressed into the magazine one at a time. Alternate magazine types, including the .22 rimfires and the Uberti Henry rifle, are loaded by pulling out the magazine tube and then dropping cartridges into the magazine one at a time. When using the rifle, the three fingers are in the lever loop, the thumb controls the hammer, and the trigger finger controls the trigger. The action must be stroked firmly and completely for proper function. The rifle must be manipulated with the butt plate firmly into the shoulder.

Working the Brooklyn Special quickly, there is one spent case in the air and the rifle back on target.

The big loop rifle looks cool, but isn't faster than any other rifle. But it is plenty fast!

BOLT-ACTION RIFLES

Sometimes called "turn bolt rifles," the bolt action usually features a fixed magazine that must be loaded with the bolt fully to the rear. Some bolt-action rifles feature a removable magazine. The bolt handle is raised in its arc, and the hand moves the bolt to the rear. Moving the bolt forward strips a cartridge from the magazine and loads the cartridge into the chamber.

Then the bolt is closed down to its original position. Proper manipulation demands that the hand not close on the bolt handle. Rather, the hand is open and the palm controls the action. The open hand rises to the bolt handle, raises the handle, the handle is pressed to the rear, and then the bolt is pressed forward and down. This type of manipulation can be very fast in good hands.

To manipulate the bolt-action rifle, the shooter begins with an open palm.

The hand sweeps up to operate the bolt.

The bolt is brought fully to the rear to eject the spent case and load another.

With practice the shooter may become proficient and fast on target with the bolt-action rifle under field conditions.

Sweeping the hand up and holding the palm open allows a shooter to manipulate the bolt-action rifle quickly. Note sling is bracing the rifle.

SELF-LOADING RIFLES

To make the self-loading rifle ready for action, the proper means is to lock the bolt to the rear. All rifles from the Century C91 to the .30 M1 Carbine load in this manner, with varia-

Quickly and smoothly operating the self-loading rifle requires an investment in training time.

tions on the bolt stop. The magazine is then inserted into the magazine well by *angling* it into the well. As the magazine locks in place, the bolt is released to run forward and load the rifle. *Never single-load a cartridge into the chamber!* The floating firing pin of the rifle is slowed down by the loading of a cartridge from the magazine. To drop the bolt on a loaded chamber is not only difficult on the extractor, but will also invite the firing pin to run forward and fire the rifle. To unload the rifle, the magazine release is actuated and the magazine removed. Next, the bolt is racked to the rear, ejecting the cartridge in the chamber. A good drill to check the chamber for a loaded cartridge is to press the rifle butt into the shoulder and then run the support hand to the chamber as the firing hand racks the bolt slightly to the rear. The support hand then feels for a cartridge in the chamber. (Hands may be reversed with some rifles.) When firing, each trigger press fires the rifle and the self-loader then loads itself.

200-Yard Zero

When using the AR-15 rifle I have adopted the 200-yard zero. This is the best all-around sighting possible. With a 2.6-inch offset over the bore line, the sights of the AR-15 would result in a cartridge striking low at close range-combat range. Even a 100-yard zero isn't the best for all-around use. Let's look at the 200-yard zero.

Range	Offset
200 yards	0
125 yards	2.5 inches high
100 yards	2.0 inches high
50 yards	0
25 yards	1.25 inches below point of aim

I used the Black Hills Ammunition 55-grain JSP to illustrate this point.

The 200-yard zero is easily the most useful zero for AR-15, Ruger Mini-14, and similar rifles. At combat range the offset is easily accounted for, and at 100 yards the same is true.

Trigger time should also include practice in manipulating the safety and magazine release.

Speed Loads

Speed loads should be practiced with your choice of rifle. The fastest speed loads are possible with the AR-15 rifle. The forefinger goes to the magazine release and hits the release, dropping the magazine. The free hand goes to the spare magazine. The magazine is angled into the magazine well. The base of the magazine is then tapped and the magazine is seated. If using the Magpul device, first grasp the magazine with the little finger and pull it out of the magazine well. Then run to the next magazine and grasp the Magpul.

There is no rifle that loads faster than an AR-15 rifle.

With one magazine falling free, the author prepares to quickly load another.

Variations may be practiced with your personal rifles, including the AK-47 or Mini-14, adapting to each magazine release.

Never use the rifle to lean against, as a walking cane, or lean a loaded rifle against a tree. The scout Kit Carson told of seeing a man grasp a rifle by the muzzle. The man had become excited as a wolf was attacking livestock. The rifle discharged and the man lost an arm. Always control the rifle and control the muzzle. When moving the rifle, keep the finger off the trigger. When the long gun is at home ready, the chamber should be empty and the magazine loaded. In the event of a home invasion, it is simple enough to rack the action and make the rifle ready. When you are searching the home or confronting a robber, the "indoor" ready stance is viable. The rifle is cradled in the arm with the muzzle down. If outside with more room, the muzzle may be higher. Inside, the muzzle should be low and pointed slightly in front of the owner. This is "indoors home ready." The rifle may be spun up and into action quickly using this drill. There is a chance the adversary may be close enough to grasp the muzzle. This is why we must be careful not to let the muzzle of the rifle clear the doorway before we clear the doorway. If the adversary grasps the muzzle the proper response is to fire. If the muzzle is not pointed at the intruder's body, for example if it is off to one side, then the best

drill is to quickly put all your weight on the rear of the rifle, lever the muzzle upward—continuing to lever the rifle up and out of the adversary's grasp—and then butt stroke him hard with the rifle butt.

The author cants the rifle to one side to clear the chamber.

The Safety

Whether you use the AR-15, a pistol-caliber carbine, or a lever-action rifle, you must practice manipulation of the safety until it is second nature. Do so in dry-fire until you cannot make a mistake.

Rapid magazine changes are an important part of malfunction drills.

Malfunction Drills

Malfunctions are rare with a properly maintained rifle using good quality magazines and ammunition. But the clearance drill must be practiced! If you have a short cycle with the AR-15, the rifle is turned on its axis with the ejection port facing down. The magazine is tapped to be certain it is seated. Then the operating rod is pulled to the rear as the rifle is shaken. The cartridge that malfunctioned should be ejected. If you have a failure to eject with a double feed, the magazine is first taken out of the rifle. If the magazine is still loaded, the magazine is kept handy to replace quickly. The bolt is racked three times rapidly to remove the stuck case from the chamber. The magazine is reinserted. Other rifles require modification to this drill, depending upon which type of operating bolt is used.

This cartridge case is inside the receiver and held fast by the bolt. In such cases, it can be difficult to clear without training.

This is a common malfunction easily cleared by those with training.

Malfunctions may be easily set up for training purposes.

CHAPTER TEN

FIRING ON THE MOVE

Too many of us spend our time firing at a static target at a preset distance. We do not move when firing, simply stand and deliver—and learn little. This is making brass, not training. We need to get moving.

The author holds his Colt at low ready.

Shooting on the move should be addressed only when you have mastered the safety requirements of the firearm. Muzzle discipline must be respected at all times. With the proper mindset, and background in safety and marksmanship, you may wish to proceed to firing on the move. Firing on the move is an important skill that allows good hits to be made at moderate ranges. The drills begin with the rifle held at low ready. You should understand *high ready*, which is the rifle held high but not aimed, and *low ready*, which is a suitable position for long-term alert and guard duty. At low ready, the rifle is held across the front of the body with the muzzle down and the firing hand in control of the rifle. When practicing moving drills, the shooter begins with a proven cadence of fire and movement. First, the shooter moves the weak side foot forward. The first step with the weak side is a long step, then a shorter step with the strong side foot. Keep the body stabilized at all times. Usually, in this type of drill you do not actually fire when moving but fire just *after* rapid movement and when movement has stopped. An important skill is to master this movement toward the target, and then stop movement and fire at a target. Begin at 10 yards and work up to 25 yards. Next, practice moving to cover and moving to

High ready isn't comfortable for long periods of time.

the rear. The strong side foot moves first to the rear in rearward movement, and then the weak side foot. The first step is always largest, followed by a short step. In other words, one leg slides to one side in a long step or sliding movement, depending upon the terrain, and the other foot moves to meet the first foot moved, resulting in smooth movement. To sidestep, move the foot on the side you wish to move first—right foot for right movement—with a larger step then a smaller step. This is a good drill to prac-tice in the home when crossing doorways as quickly as possible, and also when moving to cover. Side step, stop movement, and then fire.

Shooting while actually moving demands more discipline and practice. Begin at low ready, and hold the upper body as upright as possible with complete control of the rifle. The knees are bent to act as a shock absorber, but not excessively so. You will step with the rear foot first. This foot moves you forward in motion. You are shoving off, so to speak. As you begin to move forward the rifle comes out of low ready and into the firing position. The rifle comes to the shoulder, and you fire as soon as the sight picture is confirmed. Some practice should be taken in firing on the move. In a dynamic home invasion or takeover robbery, the ability to fire quickly and accurately on the move will be a great asset.

Rapidly covering ground with the rifle is an important and potentially lifesaving skill.

When moving, do not silhouette yourself in the middle of an area without cover.

Moving forward is sometimes called the tactical advance. This was well understood by troops in World War II. First, take a wide step forward with the weak side foot, followed by a small step with the strong side foot. Repeat this drill, and practice side steps and firing as you stop movement. Firing on the move is a last-ditch technique that should be practiced. The best use of movement is moving to a braced firing position or moving to cover. Within the confines of the home, it is important to practice movement so that you do not trip on an object. Remember, safety first. Keeping your finger off the trigger and exercising trigger discipline is critical.

When practicing on the firing range we have a tendency to stay planted to the point where we can almost grow roots. As an example, if you are awakened at night and two members of our ex-con protein-fed

Learning to quickly use the sling and fire on the move is an important skill.

criminal class are walking toward you down the hallway with handguns in hand, you do not wish to offer them a good target. At the very least, you need to sidestep to one side or the other, making for a harder target. You may be able to disappear behind a wall. If you have not mastered the basics of marksmanship, you will be hopeless when attempting to fire and move. You need to develop footwork patterns, including a lateral step away from the line of attack. Just such a simple step may confuse the adversary. The watchword is *controlled* movement. Moving backward and tripping is an uncontrolled movement that must be avoided.

Pivoting and moving quickly with the rifle may be learned only by repetition.

Quickly spinning and addressing threats from either side should be addressed.

Keeping low and maintaining a solid firing position is an important part of movement.

PRACTICE DRILL FOR SHOOTING ON THE MOVE

Begin with two targets about 10 yards apart. Begin at 7 yards. Sidestep to the right and keep moving until you have moved about 7 yards from the target to the right, then fire back to the left. This is a good beginning. You also need to consider working out at a range that provides the proper layout to conduct these drills. The drills should be done dry-fire first, but in the end you must at some point progress to live fire. Always retain muscle discipline. Practice this on the range. When performing for real, never

When moving, you should stop to properly stabilize the rifle before firing.

let the muzzle cover your body or anywhere in the home where your family is waiting for you to rescue them!

TEAMWORK

If you are in a team or a two-person defensive group in the home, team tactics should be practiced and practiced often. When practicing these tactics, the assumption might be that one part of the team is under fire. The premise is that your cover just isn't doing the job, or that you are being flanked and you need to bug out. The other team member will address the threat as you move.

There are a lot of premises and assumptions that must be made during team training, but the bottom line is that the training should be done and the training should be flexible. Split up the runs with the man on the left being the cover man, then the man on the right, and proceed from there. When performing these drills never crisscross the range with fire; that isn't safe. The right-hand shooter addresses right-hand targets, and so forth. Some training facilities will allow greater latitude in fire; most do not. When moving, the trigger finger is out of register, the safety is on, and the muzzle is down. When moving to cover with a partner, never neglect the outward peel. You move with the muzzle *away from your other shooter*. Using the outside peel during movement limits exposing the other team members to your muzzle, and is a safe means of maneuvering. The moving partner and the shooting partner should always be aware of each other.

Shooting while moving and moving to shoot, in my opinion, are defined by a well-founded desire to find cover. The threat is addressed if necessary while we are moving, but in the end the primary motivation is finding cover. All of the tactics we learn are designed to achieve this goal.

CHAPTER ELEVEN

THE IMPORTANCE OF COVER

When it comes to cover, first understand the difference between *cover* and *concealment*. Concealment could be a blanket on a clothesline or a shrub. They conceal your form, but they will not stop incoming fire. A car engine is good cover; a USPS mail box may also be. When you consider the difference between handgun cartridges and rifle cartridges, the differences between cover and effective cover is great. Rifle cartridges are powerful enough to cut through cover that would stop the most powerful handguns. When you study gunfight statistics and narratives of gunfights, one thing is certain. Those who find cover survive whether or not they are able to shoot their assailant. When approaching firing from cover, it is important we use cover but do not hug cover. Keeping an offset from cover prevents our being hit by ricochet. Keeping a certain offset makes our body silhouette smaller, and also makes it easier to quickly break from the position and move. Seeking cover is a good thing, and cover is something that offers protection from incoming fire. Remember, just because you have cover you do not have to begin firing. Sometimes the best course is to keep cover and protect your position. Unless you know where the target is and have a high likelihood of hitting the target, then you should not expose your body to incoming fire. When considering potential cover keep in mind that much of what you *thought* was cover might turn out not to be adequate. The walls inside your home are seldom cover, although brick walls may be.

Finding a braced firing position should always be a top priority.

When firing around cover do not hug cover, but rather stand back a few feet. You will minimize the chances of a ricochet or damage from a bullet strike, and your silhouette will be much smaller. A vehicle is common cover. If you use a vehicle for cover, do not lean over the hood or the top of the vehicle. Lean around the side. Use a wheel for cover. The feet are an inviting target and not difficult to hit under a car. Skipping a bullet under the car will strike your body if you are close enough. Get behind the wheel, preferably by the engine compartment. This is the only area of the car that is proof against a .30 caliber rifle. If you are close to a vehicle when the fight starts, it is good to get cover behind the vehicle. Cover is compromised once the bad guys know where you are. They may outflank you, or gain high ground and rain fire into your position.

Firing from a kneeling braced firing position offers excellent accuracy potential.

When you are using a rifle, you have a great advantage over a shotgun or handgun. The rifle is more powerful than a handgun and has greater range than a handgun. The sole disadvantage is size, length, and weight. Yet this isn't the whole story. A relatively light bolt-action rifle, such as the Remington 700 SPS or the Ruger Scout Rifle, offers a compact package that handles quickly. So does the AR-15 carbine. Handling and fast moving is an advantage. But placing yourself behind cover is another consideration. You must have the proper offset.

Quickly moving the rifle without exposing too much of the body is an important skill.

There is no sense in using a wall for cover and then hanging your body around the wall. You will probably not be in a protracted gunfight, but a gunfight that lasts but a few rounds. The tactical use of cover includes finding that cover quickly in the open, and also finding cover in the home. *The kind of cover that counts is the kind that stops a bullet. All cover is concealment, but not all concealment is cover.* When you are behind cover, you have greater control of the situation. If cover is sufficient in length and breadth you may be able to move quickly behind cover, even to the point of escaping an attack. The

You should practice firing with either hand. This may prove to be a lifesaving skill.

Learning to fire while moving and advancing on the target is an important skill.

Firing while moving to cover can be difficult to learn.

The most common cover is a vehicle. It makes sense to practice firing from vehicle cover, preferably behind a tire to prevent being hit in the leg from a shot fired under the vehicle.

Don't get married to a position, but practice rapid movement.

Getting the wheel of a vehicle behind you offers excellent bullet-stopping potential.

biggest mistake people make is crowding cover. They get too close to the covering material. You can get the body close if you are angling fire, but the rifle should be alongside the cover and little of the rifle exposed. You will have a better outlook of the area if you are offset from the cover by at least a small distance. You are less vulnerable to incoming fire or fragments. You are in a much better position to quickly move from one area to the other. This is especially true when using a vehicle for cover. Also: cover against shotgun and handgun fire isn't always effective against incoming rifle fire. A shotgun can be all encompassing, and the balls or shot may bounce around the area. A common handgun cartridge, such as the 9mm or .45 ACP, might penetrate a car door, but maybe not. If the handgun projectile strikes the door window regulator it will probably be stopped. On the other hand, a rifle cartridge will probably have sufficient power to penetrate two car doors in line and deal a lethal blow. Take this into consideration. While anything that breaks up your outline is good, most cover isn't proof against a .30 caliber rifle. An engine block or wheel house should be cover enough.

If you are offset from cover, you have a much better view of your area of fire and you will be able to break away more quickly. You limit exposure to bullet fragments from near hits. The point is that you will wish to observe and clear segments of the area in front of your sights with the least possible amount of your body exposed. At this point I am going to stress marksmanship again. For various reasons, some do not shoot well from cover. Perhaps the excitement of training or the cramped quarters affect their combat mindset. I have seen students who do not use the basics of combat marksmanship. The process takes time. Shooter development is expensive in terms of time and ammunition. We will never shoot like the Navy Seals, no matter what the man says, because we do not have the resources to train daily and fire tens of thousands of rounds in this training. Mental rehearsals, such as dry-fire and visualization techniques, are important. If you are firing from behind cover it means that you are in a fight. The lives of your family and your own will depend upon how

Firing right over the hood invites strikes from ricochets off the hood and makes for a large target.

Keeping an offset from cover makes for a smaller target.

A vehicle door isn't good cover against a rifle.

If you must use a door for cover, roll the window down; glass is hard on bullets.

well you are able to fire from behind cover. Practice taking cover, do so quickly, and fire accurately from a solid firing position.

VEHICULAR COVER

Know what bullets a vehicle will stop and which it will not. A rifle will go through most car doors, while an engine block will stop any rifle bullet. A wheel will stop most rifle projectiles.

COVER IN THE HOME

When you practice home defense, it is a valid concern to study what part of the home affords good cover. The joists and support beams of a home may be cover but only if there are several in line. It is excellent training to practice quickly assuming a firing position beside heavy

Practice firing from the barricade on the range. It will be an aid when firing in home defense.

bracing in the home, and to use this bracing both for cover and for increasing accuracy potential. A brick wall is heavy and will stop incoming fire; even the largest sofa may not. A bookcase is good cover. The average security door isn't proof against incoming fire, but could be proofed with enough effort.

A rifle with a scope may be useful at low magnification at short range; however, a LaserMax sight is an aid when firing from the barricade position.

COMBINING COVER AND CONCEALMENT

There are times when cover and concealment may be combined. Every soldier is taught to look for cover, and to utilize cover intelligently. As an example, there are fields and yards that appear to offer little to no cover, yet which, upon close examination, offer ample cover for those who both think and move quickly. A slight rise in the topography may allow the shooter to quickly roll and take advantage of bullet-stopping dirt and earth. Learning to quickly assess the situation, duck, roll, and fire from this type of cover is essential. As an example, see the next section.

COVER IN THE FIELD

An illustration shows the author behind a fallen tree that offers excellent cover. Yet, if the shooter exposes most of his body and fires over this tree then he has abrogated the advantages of this cover. Instead, a quick examination of the cover revealed an opening *under* the tree that offered an excellent opportunity for use as a firing port while the author's body was

The author has found good cover, but it is wasted in this position.

concealed. With this type of firing position available, none but the foolish would attempt a head-on assault. As a closing thought, never forget that elevation gives the aggressor an advantage. If a threat is firing from above and your body is exposed behind cover, you have lost the battle. There are times when the rule of not hugging cover too closely must be modified.

An opening under this fallen tree affords excellent cover.

A slight swell in the ground creates cover.

Sometimes you have to get down and dirty to take advantage of cover.

CHAPTER TWELVE

PRECISION RIFLE SHOOTING

AN INTEGRATION OF THE GUN AND THE SHOOTER

This chapter has two focuses: the shooter and the equipment. For long-range precision fire, the shooter and the gun must be up to the task. In this chapter I am not covering extreme long-range fire, such as the competitor who fires a 1,000-yard match or 700 yards with a special rifle, but some of the gear covered is capable of such work. Rather, we are covering placing fire accurately from 100 yards and beyond. For most of us, the practical and tactical chores encountered will stress skills that are best used inside of 300 yards. The rifle is important. The shooter is important as well, but the rifle must be up to the task. Greater tolerances mean greater chances of eccentric wear. The rifle barrel, stock, receiver, and optics are vital. I would not drive a truck with bald tires or a motorcycle with loose wheels. Similarly, the rifle cannot be loosely put together for this type of work. The rifle must also be kept clean and attention paid to tightening the stock or scope mounts if they become loose. You must maintain the proper skills in order to be able to judge your rifle's accuracy, and to notice degradation in accuracy. I have been around long enough to occasionally see a normally accurate rifle suffer some decline in accuracy. I have yet to shoot a barrel out. There were always underlying causes. As an example, a tack-driving Ruger 77 in 6.5×55mm had delivered 1 MOA on demand with Hornady Custom Light Magnum ammunition. (I had done considerable work in bedding the stock and action.) It crept up to 1.65 inches for a group. I checked the rifle and found that the scope mounts had worked loose. I tightened them and the stock, and was back in the groove. Stock screws and base nuts can become loose. Receiver screws may, as well. I am always surprised that the problem seems

The Industry Armament rifle is a precision AR-15.

to occur after a long rest in the safe! The rifle shoots well, I lock it up, and the next range has a problem with accuracy. Perhaps it was handling, or perhaps the screws came loose at the last range session. In any case, check for looseness before you fire.

Precision demands much from the rifle and the shooter, as well. The rifle action must be bedded in a good stock. Ruger rifles at one time were famed for strong actions and poor bedding, and the need for an accuracy tune-up was apparent. The rifle must be bedded to a good stock. Check the length of pull of that stock. Length of pull is the length of the trigger pull from your trigger finger pad to the rear or the stock. Too

The business card check tells a lot about wood to metal fit.

long a pull can be a detriment to practical accuracy. The barrel should be stiff and not lightweight, but need not be a heavy barrel for most uses. The scope mounts should be rigid. I have enjoyed good luck with DNZ scope mounts. With the AR-15 I have also used Talley scope mounts with excellent results. The Talley rings and mounts are a personal favorite. The rifle should be kept clean and cleaning should be consistent. There are a number of considerations with regard to the rifle. A target shooter may modify the stock for a perfect fit. A tactical shooter must have an ambidextrous rifle and stock. A benchrest-only stock isn't suitable for prone fire. On the bolt-action rifle, wooden stocks are traditional and often beautiful. However, with the modern fiberglass stock you have a stock that is strong, takes hard hits, does not crack, and is good for field use. They do not warp in bad climatic conditions. While fiberglass stocks also need to be bedded, the bedding is a relatively simple operation. With proper bedding in the bolt-action rifle, the barrel and receiver remain locked in place on firing. There is a degree of stress relieved from the barrel. (With the AR-15 a free-floating forend is needed.) Bedding the rifle simply ensures that lateral movement is eliminated and the rifle moves consistently from shot to shot. You may find a competent gunsmith to perform this task, or you may do it yourself with a kit from Brownells, together with sufficient time and study. The barreled action and stock should be glassed, including the area just ahead of the recoil lug and the back recoil lug area and tang.

The Hiperfire trigger, lower, is an excellent addition to any rifle.

Sometimes it helps to relieve contact points. As an example, some years ago the Ruger Mini-14 was regarded as less accurate than the Colt AR-15. I didn't expect a super accurate rifle after experience with the .30 carbine. But 3–4-inch groups at 100 yards did not impress. Both the sights and the bedding are improved in modern guns. The Ruger Mini-14 is more of a miniature M14 rifle than an upsized .30 carbine. However, I used an old trick I had used with the .30 carbine. I relieved the area around the gas block on the Ruger. It had been in contact with the stock. This simple expedient reduced aver-age group sizes to 2–3 inches

This rifle features DNZ scope mounts and a Redfield scope.

with the Hornady 55-grain FMJ training load. Rifles are individuals, but some experience crosses over to the next rifle.

The term "free-floating" simply means that the barrel does not touch any part of the barrel inlet in the stock. The channel in the stock is larger than the barrel diameter. The barrel cools better and is harmonically damp-ened when it does not touch the stock. This also prevents buildup of oil and solvent between the barrel and stock. A refresher on the length of pull: the tip of the trigger finger is all that is needed to be on the trigger. The inside crease of the arm to the crease of the tip of the trigger finger is the usual measure. You must be able to exert pressure on the trigger straight to the rear. Bedding and length of pull are important factors in a true long-range rifle. Accuracy is more than one part of the rifle, but a sum of the parts all properly put together.

HARDWARE

We will discuss optics in a later chapter. A strong rule is that the scope mounts and rings must be strong and capable of taking the stress of firing after each shot without allowing a deviation in the scope's position. The scope mount must be of first-class construction. At present the DNZ type rides on two hard-use rifles, the Remington 700 .308 and the Colt AR-15 5.56mm. I have enjoyed excellent results with the Talley mount on both a Mossberg Patrol Rifle and another AR-15 rifle. These mounts have given excellent service. The rails mount on the receiver and are best in a one-piece base. Rings must be a good fit for the mount and the scope. Poor quality rings must be avoided.

Aperture sights have excellent accuracy potential inside of 100 yards.

Breaking in the rifle is an arcane subject that is often discussed among experienced shooters. Both breaking in the rifle barrel and proper cleaning become much more important when the range exceeds 200 yards. As long as you clean the rifle properly and do not run the rifle until it is hot and smoking, you are fine in breaking in a new barrel. I think that some claims of a prodi-

These are factory Colt M4 sights. They are useful for accurate fire well past 200 yards.

gious number of rounds fired in a single weekend shooting outing should be taken with a grain of salt. A few hundred rounds are sufficient to cause the AR-15 rifle to smoke and become too hot to hold. Three to four hundred rounds in a single hour could cause the rifle to reach a temperature of up to 400 degrees. Much more, if you could stand to hold the rifle while firing these cartridges, and permanent barrel damage might occur. With the .308 bolt action, I do not think we will approach this number of cartridges. There are lapping kits that are designed to smooth up the barrel. While reputable and sometimes worthwhile, fire lapping has questionable value, in my opinion, for high-quality modern rifles. Most are well polished just as they are

One of the author's favorite combinations is the Redfield Battle zone and DNZ scope mounts.

Firing the Remington .308 off the benchrest with the Redfield scope gave excellent results.

The Redfield Battle zone isn't expensive, but it has given good results.

delivered. Still, I have developed a break-in procedure that is neither original nor particularly difficult, but which seems to benefit most rifles.

Begin with a Clean Barrel

Fire a shot, clean the barrel. Then fire five shots and clean the barrel, repeating for about forty rounds. This is how I do it.

How to Properly Clean the Rifle Barrel

I am very careful with the muzzle, rifle grooves, and lands. Sure, they take a beating, but damage is more likely with a poorly designed cleaning rod than a copper-plated bullet. Use a cleaning rod that is coated, and which offers good control as you guide the rod down the barrel. A rotating handle is good to have. The brush will follow the twists of the barrel when a rotating handle is used. A non-rotating handle jumps the lands. For cleaning solutions, Hoppe's No. 9 is the classic and it works as well as ever. I have also used a number of new formulations from Sharp Shoot R with excellent results. The Sharp Shoot R formula is citrus based and is less offensive when used indoors. Use the Dewey's bore guide to guide the rod into the barrel without damaging the lands or grooves. Patches should be cotton based. Use the proper size, or even a trimmed patch, to avoid putting excess pressure on the rod. If the rod is stressed it will stick or bend. Uncoated bore rods will possibly scratch the barrel. In order to properly clean the barrel, I first use a heavily soaked patch first. The bore solvent will attack lead and copper deposits, as well as powder ash. I use two patches. Next I use the brass brush and twist the bore brush through the barrel and back. Ten to a dozen swipes with the bore brush in the barrel will usually clean the barrel. Then use a cotton patch that is lightly soaked in solvent, and finally a dry patch. The dry patch should come away clean. For storage, the final step is to run a patch soaked with oil through the barrel.

The Nikon M-223 is a great all-around optic for the AR-15 rifle. Note sturdy mount.

The Precision AR

When it comes to the AR-15 rifle there are a few things that must be supported. The AR-15 is well suited to long-range use, and also long-range rapid fire use. A good quality AR-15 may be termed a Dedicated Marksman's Rifle, as that is the military equivalent. I sometimes shudder at the thought process of some who seek to build such a rifle and then feed it junk ammunition. You cannot expect a good quality rifle to perform with steel case or bottom basement loads. Also remember that, for the most part, an expanding bullet is irrelevant at long range. We are primarily shooting paper. At long range, few JSP bullets will exhibit meaningful expansion unless they are designed from the outset as long-range bullets. The best bullets for long-range accuracy with the .223 begin with the 69-grain Nosler. The 77-grain Nosler has proven quite accurate given proper load practice in handloads. While factory ammunition is often very accurate, the only way to achieve real proficiency at arms is to load your own and to do so properly and carefully. Economy demands handloading. You will also wish to use a longer, heavier barrel than the standard 16-inch carbine. A heavy barrel rifle is the superior option. A rule of thumb is that, once the .223 projectile slips below 2,500 fps, wound potential is reduced to the unreliable point. The heavy barrel rifle with a longer tube increases the potential for effective use of the .223 caliber. If the target is a predator, such as a coyote, then the effective range is far past the effective range for critical use. Varmint range is the range at which you can hit the animal. Thin barrels heat up more quickly. If you are shooting varmints, or engaging in long practice sessions, the heavier barrels are better. The hand guard must be free-floated. If the barrel doesn't float free, then the key harmonics are ruined. In top flight accuracy at over 100 yards, only free-floated barrels need apply. You will need to retrofit a rifle without a free-floating barrel if your accuracy project begins with this type of rifle. Better to purchase a modern rifle with free-floating barrel. The rifle stock should be adjustable. When you are taking every advantage for an accurate first shot hit, then the rifle stock means a lot. Magpul, Mission First Tactical, and Hogue offer first class stocks with excellent features. The comfort of the shooter is important in long-range fire. The cheekweld, hold, and trigger reach all add up to a combination that makes for more accurate shooting. Be certain you mate the stock to the optics as well, since this makes a difference. It is difficult to make accurate shots if the stock doesn't fit your body. You need a good quality AR-15 trigger with a clean break of four pounds. for a precision rifle. There are lighter weight triggers, but it takes a great marksman to use them properly. A two-stage trigger is best for precision work. The single-stage trigger is great for fast work and multiple

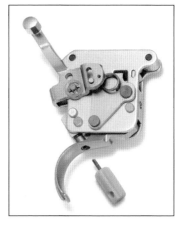

An aftermarket trigger can be an aid in managing the trigger for long-range fire.

The ATN X-Sight is a marvel of modern optics.

Storm Tactical record books are an essential tool for keeping up with performance and evaluating the precision rifle.

targets, while the two-stage is still best for off the bench or braced work. In the end, the shooter is the most important component, but the rest of the rifle is pretty important as well.

Match-Grade Loads

Match-grade ammunition is terribly important for real precision. Although I handload, I have the greatest respect for carefully crafted factory loads. Do I always equal or beat factory loads? When it comes to match-grade factory loads, I am in the running and that is all. Also, when it comes to Creedmoor ammunition, the price is reasonable when you consider that this ammunition is put up in fifty-round boxes, not the usual twenty-round boxes. Divide the price in half and you have the typical price of a twenty-round box of MATCH loads, but half of the Creedmoor package is twenty-five rounds. Creedmoor offers the 69-grain Sierra TMK at 2,850 fps. This is a load that will do 99 percent of what any of us need to do with a rifle. It takes an excellent rifle to show the advantage of this load, but the average rifle will also prove more accurate. For those who engage in long-range use of the .223 Remington, the 75-grain HPBT is a credible choice. My custom grade AR-15 is mostly Spikes Tactical, and a recent addition is the Wisconsin Trigger Milazzo-Krieger Two-Stage trigger. I was surprised if not amazed at the accuracy potential of this loading. This load breaks a lot of rules by staying in the same hole well past 100 yards, at least when I do my part. The 77-grain MatchKing offered by Creedmoor is another classic. I have not invested as much time in this load, as the human component is what must be addressed, in my opinion, to better the performance of my most accurate rifle. For longest range, my suggestion would be to use this load.

First-class match-grade loads from Creedmoor up the ante for accuracy.

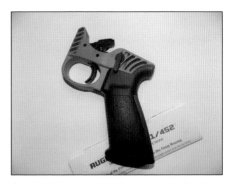

Ruger offers a special trigger upgrade for the AR 556 that comes in a polymer grip frame.

The Creedmoor .308 Winchester MATCH loads are put up in Lapua brass and use the 167-grain Scenar bullet. Quite simply, this is a match made in heaven. The Lapua website spells out the success of the Scenar bullet, which holds the IBS World Record in 600-yard heavy gun five-shot groups at an amazing 0.404 inch. The official ISSF record of 600 cannot be bested and was shot with the Scenar. My personal rifle is a Remington 700, and is probably not the best platform for accuracy testing. But results with a three-shot group were well under 1 MOA, some much better.

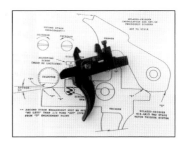

The Wisconsin Trigger Company offers what may be the premier trigger for precision use.

If the iron is up to it, this combination will deliver precision. The Creedmoor .30-06 Springfield load also uses the Scenar bullet. This is the single most accurate loading I have fired in the Garand rifle. With a properly tuned rifle the results should be excellent. To put up your own match-grade loads, you simply have to be consistent, carefully weigh each powder charge, and be certain that you have taken time to select a premium bullet.

StraightJacket

I have used a fascinating piece of equipment on my personal Ruger M77 rifle that I feel is more than effective in dissipating heat, and also in improving accuracy. The StraightJacket Barrel System covers the original barrel with a cover that has the appearance of a heavy barrel, but which is lighter. The StraightJacket adds about 24 ounces on average to a rifle. The barrel is bonded to the StraightJacket and the inner material (a proprietary mix that may be powdered metal or gel, I do not know which, but it works) is between the jacket and the original barrel. The barrel is what is called in industrial terms a "heat sink." It works and works well. There is little flex in the barrel. The StraightJacket allows the firing of ammunition in greater quantity and with greater rapidity of fire than any other rifle I am aware of. The jacket heats up but the chamber feels cool. Accuracy does not decline with a long firing string. Teludyne's StraightJacket really works. My Ruger M77 has turned in groups of less than 0.6 inch at a long 100 yards with the Black Hills Ammunition 168-grain MATCH hollowpoint. I have also fired the rifle at 200 yards, and frankly I have been very surprised. I think that for extensive long-range work I should change to the 175-grain Black Hills MATCH load, but with a 1.5-inch 200-yard group from this relatively light rifle, I have no complaint.

The author's StraightJacket Ruger proved deadly accurate.

The StraightJacket barrel system met its advertised performance.

Not everyone likes the appearance of the StraightJacket, no getting around that, but for those who feel a need for greater accuracy potential in any climatic condition, this is the trick. I enjoy my rifle very much. I think that the perfect application would be for a varmint hunter who loves to shoot and shoots a lot. I began testing the rifle with an inexpensive scope that give up shooting at about 60 rapid fire rounds. The Meopta 3–9×40mm scope fitted to the rifle is an ideal companion. The glass is clear, adjustments are excellent, and the rifle and scope combination unbeatable.

CHAPTER THIRTEEN

LEVER-ACTION RIFLES

When it comes to personal defense and the tools for the job, we are in agreement as to what is appropriate. The handgun is the weapon of opportunity, always carried with us. The long gun is the best choice when we have a warning of danger. If we choose to have a firearm ready in the home, then it should be a long gun. There are jurisdictions in the United States that make it difficult to own and use a handgun. While such people's republics place the power of the state above the safety of the people, packing up and moving is easier said than done for many of our brothers and sisters. That is where the Brooklyn Special becomes an option.

The Brooklyn Special is a rifle I have seen many times, and a term I have heard so often the origins are lost to my memory. Suffice to say, the Brooklyn Special is a light, handy carbine designed

The humble lever-action rifle has many advantages for a modern shooter.

for home defense. Pushed to the limits of the type, it is also a good choice for traveling or for use in a civil emergency. The most common iteration of the type is a lever-action carbine. The caliber may be what we term a "pistol-caliber," such as the .357 Magnum, or a "rifle-caliber," such as the .30-30 WCF. In either case the carbine offers more power and accuracy, and faster handling, than any handgun. The Brooklyn Special kicks less than a 12-gauge shotgun and is suitable for taking game in an emergency. In short, this is a firearm with much to recommend.

While politically correct isn't always at the top of our list, it sometimes is by necessity. The Brooklyn Special is as politically acceptable as any firearm can be by virtue of its traditional appearance. I own several rifles that may be called Brooklyn Specials. I have also helped friends and family build their own versions. Each is tailored to suit one taste or the other, and each is effective in the hands of the person deploying the rifle. The rules are simple: fixed sights, lever action, lightweight, hits hard. As a rule breaker, I have experimented with is the Henry rifle in .22 Long Rifle. For a young person or anyone on a strict budget, the Henry lever-action .22 meets all criteria for a Brooklyn Special, save power. While not usually included in the genre, a .22 caliber lever-action rifle that will place three Winchester Dyna Point bullets into 2 inches at 50 yards must be respected. Most of us will choose a pistol-caliber lever-action rifle. The advantages of the pistol calibers are many. First, let's get something out of the way. The Winchester "dash" rounds, such as the .32 DASH 20, the .38-40, and the .44-40, were conceived as rifle cartridges. They were then adapted to revolvers. These semi bottlenecked cartridges were good choices in their day, but there are better choices in this century. The .44-40 is in simple terms a 10mm Auto in power. It is useful but requires handloads to achieve its full measure of effectiveness. It is a great cartridge, and if you own granddad's Winchester 92 you have a fine rifle. If you are ordering a new Puma, the .44 Magnum is more practical.

The Rossi pistol-caliber carbine offers excellent leverage for short pistol cartridges.

The Rossi carbine has well fitted and strong locking lugs.

The lever-action rifle use an action modified from the Volcanic lever-action rifle by Henry and perfected by Winchester. (The original toggle lock later showed up in the Maxim machine gun and the Luger pistol. It is a respected engineering marvel.) Later lever-action rifles use a far more efficient action than the Winchester 1866, beginning with the big bore 1886 rifle and later the Winchester 1892. The pistol-caliber carbines with their short cartridges have greater leverage than the .30-30 WCF, .35 Remington and other bottle neck rifle cartridges. As a result, rapidity of fire is greater. While few of us foresee a running gun battle, the pistol-caliber carbine offers a rapid backup shot if need be. The Puma rifle in .357 Magnum features thirteen rounds in its tubular magazine. The carbine version holds ten rounds. And while I do not foresee having to reload during a home defense situation, if you mount an ammo carrier on the stock you may top the magazine off by simply thumbing rounds into the loading gate one at a time.

The .357 Magnum lever-action rifle works just fine with .38 Special ammunition, and the .44 Magnum works well with .44 Special loads. Either caliber is acceptable for home defense situations. The carbine is more accurate and offers faster handling than any handgun. This greatly increases the potential for stopping an opponent with a single well-placed shot. Accuracy can make up for power; the reverse is seldom true. Barrel lengths of 16–24 inches are available in the pistol-caliber carbines. The short barrel lengths are faster to handle in close quarters. The longer lengths are well suited to game shooting, and some compromise may be needed to find the perfect rifle for your needs. The traditional buckhorn sights are fine for hunting, but you may wish to add a set of the excellent XS aperture sights. I have fitted a set to one of my personal Winchester Model 94 rifles. This sight combination gives excellent results in speed shooting to 50 yards or so. I have also fitted a Providence Tool sight, a reproduction of the original Lyman sight, to one of my Trapper carbines. While fast into action, this sight offers real precision and easy adjustment for long-range shooting. My example of the Winchester Trapper is in .30-30 WCF. Winchester Trapper carbines are sometimes found in .44 Magnum but they are becoming scarce.

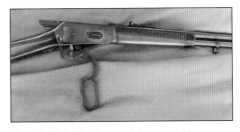

The .30-30 WCF offers useful power with a longer action.

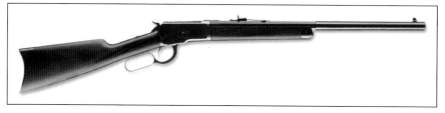

Winchester's Model 1892 rifle is back in production. It isn't inexpensive but certainly offers a great deal of pride of ownership.

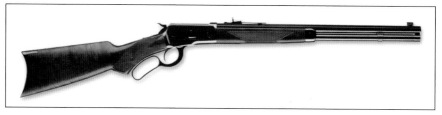

Winchester's High Grade lever-action rifles are first-class rifles in every way.

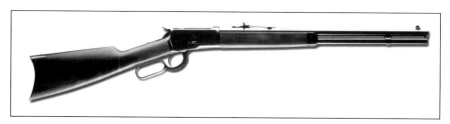

The plain Jane lever-action rifle is useful for many chores.

For most of us the various Rossi/Puma rifles are the best choice. Well-made of good material, these rifles are accurate and seem to be trouble free. A warning: avoid the cool looking big ring levers. John Wayne used one in the movies, sure, and I am not certain where the big ring lever originated. The proven technique in using a lever-action rifle is to press the lever forward, not downward. Using this technique with a fast-handling pistol-caliber carbine allows a very rapid follow-up shot that is not possible with a big ring lever. Since the cadence of fire is set by how fast you are able to acquire the sights after recoil, more than how quickly you are able to lever the action and press the trigger, good technique with the lever-action rifle makes for excellent speed with follow-up shots.

This is a modern high grade Winchester 1894 rifle in .30-30 WCF.

When studying the lever-action rifle, the advantages of a rifle with an exposed hammer are apparent. I recommend leaving the rifle chamber empty when at ready. The rifle may be charged quickly by racking the lever. If you are not ready to fire, simply lower the hammer. The hammer may be cocked quickly. It is a simple matter to unload the chamber by camming the cartridge out, but doing so without loading another cartridge requires some practice. The modern Rossi features a safety on the bolt that wasn't found on the original Model 92. Do not remove it by any means, but use it or ignore it as you see fit. I ignore the safety on my Rossi, and keep my head clear and safety first when using any firearm. My personal Puma is chambered for the .357 Magnum cartridge. The wound potential of the .357 Magnum cartridge is well known, and even greater when fired from a rifle. The carbine magnifies the power of the pistol's cartridge by virtue of a full powder burn. A surplus of two hundred to three hundred feet per second is realized. A misconception is that this increased velocity results in less penetration, and even bullet fragmentation. Underpenetration was a concern before the introduction of modern bullets, such as the Hornady XTP. When firing a number of cartridges using the XTP bullet I observed that, while velocity increased substantially, both expansion and penetration were increased as well. This was particularly true with the Black Hills 158-grain JHP load using the XTP, and handloads using the 180-grain XTP. As long as you do not choose one of the frangible 110-grain bullets, the carbine should give you a full measure of the cartridge's power. I have read warnings that traditional cup-and-core-type JHP bullets may lose their jacket in the .357 carbine's barrel. I have

The Winchester 1895 takedown is chambered for powerful cartridges, such as the .30-40 and .270 WCF. It is more specialized than most lever-action rifles.

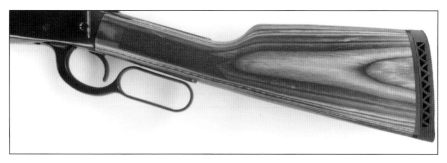

Lever-action rifles may be customized. This is a Boyd's rifle stock with butt pad for the Winchester 92/Rossi lever-action.

not experienced this problem because I have not used lightweight bullets. The 158-grain JHP isn't always the top choice for a revolver because the penetration is on the long end and expansion is less than we would like for personal defense. With the carbine, this isn't the case. Loads using the 158-grain XTP are probably the best all-around choice. For deer-sized game the Hornady 140-grain FTX is an option.

This brings us to an important point. Carbines are carbines and revolvers are revolvers. Owning a revolver and a carbine chambered for the same cartridge is a convenience, but not a necessity. The way they behave with certain loads differs. Contrary to popular belief, my experience indicates that a rifle will not handle a heavier load than a handgun; when it comes to Ruger handguns the opposite may be true. They are different firearms types and must be treated as such. The Puma .357 is one Brooklyn Special that is accurate far beyond typical personal defense ranges. As an example, when firing off a solid benchrest at a long 50 yards this rifle will produce a three-shot 2-inch group with the Black Hills 158-grain JHP. With the rear sight at its lowest setting, the rifle is dead-on at 100 yards with this capable load. For practice sessions, loads using either hard-cast lead bullets or plated bullets offer good accuracy. There is simply little to criticize in this rifle. I have also used the Puma in .44 Magnum with good results. This rifle is not quite as accurate as the .357 Magnum, but is equally as reliable. With the .44 Magnum, an excellent home defense load would be the Winchester .44 Special PDX, or the 215-grain .44 Magnum Winchester Silvertip for greater power. The Hornady 200-grain XTP is a great load for thin-skinned game, while the Hornady 240-grain XTP offers excellent penetration. Choose the load based on your personal scenario. The .454 Casull version of the Puma is certainly a contender. Standard .45 Colt loads may be used in the Puma .454. The .45 Colt is my least favorite pistol-caliber carbine cartridge, but the .45 Colt works just fine in the Puma. If defense against large animals is a real concern, the .454 Puma probably offers more punch per pound than any other rifle in this class. Recoil becomes a consideration at this power level.

The Lyman aperture sight was added to the Winchester 92 with excellent results.

There are many alternatives to handguns for home defense. The superiority of the long gun isn't up for discussion. The pistol-caliber lever gun is simpler and more reliable in a worst-case scenario than a self-loader in a pistol caliber. The lever-action calibers are straight across the board more powerful than the semiautomatic calibers, such as the 9mm, .40 and .45 ACP. The centerfire caliber Brooklyn Special is lighter and easier to handle than any other centerfire rifle. There are three types of pistol-caliber carbines in general use. There are purpose-designed self-loaders, such as the Beretta Storm, the Kel-Tec, and the High Point. The pistol-caliber lever-action rifle is probably the best suited to personal defense for most of us. I appreciate my lever-action carbines, and if you give the type an honest evaluation so will you.

Top to bottom: Savage 99 .308 with Marble aperture sight, Winchester .32-20 with Lyman aperture sight, and Marlin 39A .22. All are useful hunting rifles.

ACCURACY RESULTS, BROOKLYN SPECIAL

Puma .44 Magnum Carbine, 50 yards, three-shot groups			
.44 Special		.44 Magnum	
Hornady 180-gr. XTP	2.2 inches	Fiocchi 240-gr. XTP	2.0 inches
Federal 225-gr. SWCHP	3.0 inches	Federal American Eagle 240-gr. JSP	2.5 inches

Marlin .44 Magnum Carbine, 50 yards, three-shot groups			
Black Hills 240-gr. JHP	2.0 inches	Speer 270-gr. Gold Dot	2.25 inches
Fiocchi 240-gr. XTP	2.5 inches	Winchester 250-gr. Silvertip	3.0 inches

Puma .357 Magnum, 50 yards, three-shot groups			
.38 Special		.357 Magnum	
Winchester 130-gr. FMJ	3.8 inches	Hornady 125-gr. XTP	2.0 inches
Hornady 125-gr. XTP	3.5 inches	Fiocchi 158-gr. JHP	1.8 inches

Rifle caliber lever-action (scoped rifle), 50-yard groups					
Marlin Model 336 .30-30		Winchester Model 94 (20-inch barrel/XS sights)		Winchester Trapper (16-inch barrel, Providence Tool Lyman sight)	
Federal Fusion 150-gr.	0.75 inch	Winchester 150-gr. Power Point	2.5 inches	Winchester 150-gr. Power Point	1.5 inches
Hornady 160-gr. LEVERevolution	0.65 inch	Federal Fusion 150-gr. JSP	2.0 inches	Federal Fusion 150-gr.	1.25 inches

The .30-30 WCF, top, is more powerful than the .357 Magnum, lower, but the revolver cartridge is useful within 100 yards.

CHAPTER FOURTEEN

AMMUNITION SELECTION AND SUPPLY

You have your rifle; now you have to feed it. Within the broad area of ammunition choices there are several levels of performance to expect from each cartridge. Bulk or inexpensive ammunition is suitable for most of our informal practice. Highly developed hunting loads do a great job in each caliber. Personal defense loads are available in most rifle calibers. I have divided my choices, and the loads I stock for my personal rifles, into three categories. The first is practice/training. These will typically be FMJ loads in the .223 and .308. These loads are

A stack of magazines and good ammunition makes for good training!

reliable and clean burning, and while some are quite accurate they are not as accurate as most of the service loads. My handloads for training figure into this category, and so does the Black Hills Ammunition remanufactured line and Winchester USA. These loads will constitute about 95 percent of what I fire

every year. Next will come hunting loads. I use these in just a few calibers. The Hornady Full Boar .223 load or the Hornady A-MAX .308 are good examples of proper hunting loads for rifles. In personal defense, I have settled upon a few proven numbers. In .223 the Black Hills Ammunition 77-grain OSM is one. The Nosler 64-grain JHP shows great promise. Before you choose ammunition, you will choose a rifle, and before you

This is just one reason why the author isn't mad about steel cased ammunition! Less than perfect storage can cause rust.

choose a rifle you will choose the caliber. When choosing a caliber there are many good efficient cartridges. You must consider all potential uses, and the availability of the cartridge, as well. As an example, I am a fan of the .300 Savage rifle cartridge. Just the same, I would never seek out a rifle for personal use chambered in this cartridge as my only rifle. The reason: The .300 Savage will not do anything the .308 Winchester will not do, and the .308 is readily available at every retail outlet. The same may be said for a number of very useful rifle cartridges. The .257 Roberts is a great cartridge, but it isn't stocked by many shops. Ammunition replenishment is an important consideration. There is also the consideration of having enough gun for the job. If you are hunting medium-skinned game to 200 yards, the .308 Winchester is a great all-around

Winchester's affordable USA line is a great training resource.

choice. The .30-06 Springfield offers a useful increase in power. But when we increase power over the .308 we are getting into a less useful type of rifle. The "go anywhere, do anything" rifle perhaps should be a .308 Winchester. The three most useful cartridges in America, in my opinion, are the .22 Long Rifle, the .223 Remington, and the .308 Winchester. An argument may be made for many others, but in the end these three will serve well. Three cartridges and three rifles will solve most of the problems you are likely to encounter. Remember, this book is a guideline for beginning. If you wish to later add specialized cartridges and handload that is a fine thing to do. But the young man in Ocala, Florida, depending upon store-bought ammunition may have a different opinion. I have included accurate knowledge. There is a danger of importing philosophy into research. I have done much research. Originality has not been gained at the expense of truth. Usefulness is important, and I

HPR offers good ammunition in a wide variety of configuration for training, hunting, and personal defense.

have formed my opinions on personal experience and a wealth of data that has contributed to my understanding. Only with firsthand knowledge may a commentator contribute to greater understanding. Opinions fly, and are a distraction rather than a help in choosing a cartridge for important uses. Let's sow with the hand, not the pen.

.22 LONG RIFLE

The typical .22 LR load is a Winchester 40-grain RNL bullet at 1255 fps. By dropping the weight to 37 grains, about 30 fps is gained in the Winchester Super X hollowpoint. Storing five hundred rounds of .22 LR is as easy as storing fifty rounds of just about anything else. The .22 LR will be found in the most out-of-the-way places that stock any type of ammunition. In a quality rifle such as the Ruger 10/22, the cartridge will serve as a formidable all-around small game and personal defense combination. The cartridge features a relatively low report. The .22 is inexpensive, and even the best rifles are relatively inexpensive as well. For these reasons the .22 LR is the best trainer we are going to use. But the .22 LR is also useful for small game. Rabbit, squirrel, and birds will fall to a well-placed .22 LR bullet. For food and foraging the .22 is a great choice. Let's face it: no matter what the major caliber rifle you end up with, you need to start with the .22 and keep the .22. As for the preservation of life in personal defense, the .22 LR is a far better cartridge from the rifle than from the handgun. In my files are no fewer than six instances in which a single 40-grain solid laid out a total of four burglars and two assailants, each with a single shot, and with four fatalities. There are also failures, but the man on a budget who practices isn't naked before his enemies with a good .22. The .22 rifle is easy to use well. Accuracy is excellent. The cartridge itself exhibits sufficient penetration for personal defense, at least with standard loads.

As for hunting, untold number of small game have been taken with the .22 LR. Hunting red-tailed squirrel with a .22 is similar to hunting moose with a .50 caliber rifle! The bullet takes game cleanly and doesn't damage too much meat. I think that the .22 may be taxed by larger game, such as fox and coyote, but if it is all you have you simply have to shoot straight. Predators are not game animals, but we still wish to give them a

For most uses the 69-grain Tipped MatchKing is an outstanding bullet. Black Hills Ammunition offers first-class ammunition.

humane death. Possum and raccoon may fall to the .22 and a keen marksman. I am going to make a recommendation for ammunition that may seem simplistic, but then this is a simple and effective cartridge. My larder is filled with the 40-grain RNL loading. For small game and practice these loads, purchased in

Winchester's M22 load in a .22 LR is specifically intended for use in self-loading rifles.

Fiocchi's .22 LR ammunition is more often than not match-grade accurate. Quality is high.

bulk, are the ideal choice. The RNL bullet deforms a bit on the nose in ballistic testing as much as the typical hollow-point. I find the light fast bullets are often less accurate. The Winchester 40-grain RNL or Fiocchi' s 40-grain RNL, each ordered in high velocity form, are the usual choice. I keep on hand a few Winchester Super X hollow-points "just in case," but find the 40-grain RNL does anything I need to do. This is the cartridge you cannot do without.

.22 MAGNUM

I find the .22 Magnum superior to the .17s for many reasons. The lighter .17 bullets are great for varmints at short range. But if you are going to go after heavier animals that the .22 LR cannot handle, I prefer the .22 Magnum. If you have shot crows with folded wings, you know what I am referring to. Good penetration is demanded. The .17 is quite accurate, and so is the .22 Magnum. With either you may make a hit past the sure killing range, something to consider when taking on larger small game. The .22 Magnum will jolt a 40-grain bullet to about 2,000 fps. The Fiocchi 40-grain JSP has given excel-

The .22 Magnum is a useful cartridge for small game.

lent results in several rifles. In this rifle, I find the lighter bullets a "sometimes" useful combination. The Hornady 30-grain V-Max will break 2,300 fps from a full-length rifle. This is a great varmint load at closer ranges. The primary difficulty with the .22 Magnum at present is ammunition availability. Stores are non-existent in my area.

The humble cartridge means a lot to the man on the point. Black Hills Ammunition offers ammunition you may reasonably bet your life on.

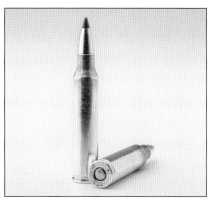

Black Hills Tipped MatchKing is a credible loading for all-around use.

During a shortage, the .22 Magnum seems to be the cartridge that is curtailed in production first. The .22 Magnum rifle is available primarily in bolt-action and lever-action rifles.

.30 CARBINE

When I first became a peace officer, the .30 carbine was carried in many patrol cars. The average World War II carbine would group three shots into 5–6 inches at 100 yards. The clones and copies are not particularly good quality and should be avoided. The modern Auto-Ordnance carbine is an exception. This is a well-made and reliable rifle with good accuracy potential, about 4 inches at 100 yards in stock form. The carbine is light, handy, and makes an excellent truck and home defense gun. It is highly specialized; however, I would prefer it to any of the 5.7mm PDW firearms. Typical ballistics are 110 grains at 1900 fps. The FMJ loads are useful for practice. Winchester is usually the most accurate FMJ loading; others are useful for practice. The Hornady 100-grain FTX is the newest and predictably the most effective expanding bullet load. I prefer other rifles, but the .30 carbine is worth a look.

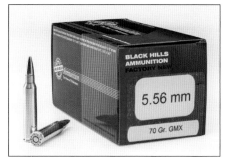

Black Hills Ammunition offers a wide range of loads for special purpose use.

7.62X39MM

This is the cartridge fired by the AK-47 rifle, and is by any standard a formidable cartridge. It is available primarily in the AK platform, with AR and bolt-action rifles also chambered for this cartridge. It was developed during World War II and was chambered in the AK-47 rifle by 1947. This is a compact cartridge with good intermediate performance. The cartridge is a true short full power cartridge, rather than a straight walled cartridge case such as the .30 carbine. The shoulder angle is similar to the .308 Winchester. The case is only 1.53 inches long. The standard loading is a 123-grain FMJ bullet at 2,350 fps. The Russian cartridge has a reputation as an inaccurate number best suited to spray and pray tactics. This isn't completely true. Most AK-47 rifles will group three shots into 4–6.5 inches at 100 yards. Some are more accurate and, with poorly made aftermarket furniture, some are worse. There are many affordable loads available in this caliber, mostly Russian-made steel cased loads. Increased penetration and a larger projectile are advantages of the 7.62×39mm over the 5.56mm NATO, but so is low cost. A case of one thousand rounds goes a long way. At present, the recommended loading for the 7.62×39mm for personal defense and game is the Hornady 123-grain SST. Some caution should be used if this caliber is to be chosen for

Hornady's 55-grain FMJ training ammunition is clean burning, accurate and, most of all, reliable.

home defense, because the 7.62×39mm has much greater penetration with FMJ loads than the .223 Remington. The 7.62×39mm cartridge is adequate for wild boar and deer-sized game at moderate ranges. If you are looking for gilt-edged accuracy this isn't the cartridge. If you are in search of utility, wound ballistics, penetration, and relatively inexpensive ammunition, the 7.62×39mm cartridge is a winner. In bolt-action Czech rifles, the cartridge ballistically equals the .30-30 Winchester.

.300 BLACKOUT

This is a relatively new number. The .300 Blackout is similar to the JD Jones-developed .300 Whisper. The cartridge is a necked-up .221 Fireball intended to offer subsonic ammunition for suppressed platforms. The cartridge was also intended to offer superior wound ballistics to suppressed 9mm firearms. With a 220-grain .308 bullet that tumbles in ballistic media, the baseline was met. The .300 Blackout will approach the performance of 7.62×39mm loads. The platform is more accurate than an AK-47 type rifle. The cartridge is reliable and

This is the Federal 62-grain FMJ loading. The Green Tip is among the most accurate of FMJ loads.

useful in the AR-15 conversions. A barrel change is all that is needed to convert your AR-15 to .300 Blackout. The 7.62×39mm on average may exhibit 150 to 200 fps more velocity in similar length barrels. However, the design of the .300 BAC allows a bullet with greater ballistic coefficient. Those loving the .300 BAC will point out that at 200 yards the .300 BAC catches up to the 7.62×39mm; but not many of us will be firing the Soviet cartridge for accuracy at that range. The .300 BAC is another matter. In the end the .300 BAC is a specialized cartridge. Those wishing to use a medium power cartridge at long range find it attractive. For suppressed rifles, which is beyond the scope of this book, the cartridge is far ahead of the 7.62×39mm. For close-range shootouts the Soviet cartridge seems better, but the .300 BAC isn't bad. The load is becoming more available, with Black Hills offering the .300 Whisper, Fiocchi offering good FMJ loads, and Gorilla Ammunition offering a variety of loads.

5.56MM/.223 REMINGTON OPTIONS

The .223 Remington is America's cartridge, just as the AR-15 rifle is America's rifle. This rifle is used for recreational shooting, competition, varmint hunting, medium game hunting, and personal defense. The same rifle will handle all of these chores, given a skilled shooter. While the rifle is versatile and may fill each role well, no single loading will serve in every pursuit. The most versatile loads may perform well in two or three roles, but I find that specialization is an aid when it comes to satisfaction with the rifle. There are highly specialized loads such as the Black Hills Ammunition Varmint

Left to right: Black Hills, Hornady, and Federal loads. Each offers good but different performance.

Grenade, and others such as the Black Hills 60-grain V-Max that are versatile. Let's take a look at some of the better choices. It isn't possible to cover every choice, but we may be able to get the rifleman started in the right direction. The loads enumerated have been test fired in the author's Colt, Daniel Defense, and Ruger rifles. A number were also fired in a long-serving Bushmaster carbine.

Recreation

I would wager that over 90 percent of the .223 rounds fired in America are fired in recreational use, in low stress pursuits. That is true at my house. I have fired my old alarm and excursion Colt HBAR for fun, at varmints, and at distant targets often over the past twenty years. I have settled into the bench in pursuit of MOA accuracy. I have practiced tactical drills. But, it was enjoyable. In the event the rifle is called on for real, I am, fortunately, familiar with its capabilities. For recreational shooting the best choice is the least expensive quality ammunition available. We all have brand loyalty and Winchester USA and Federal American Eagle may be found for a similar price, but sometimes one or the other may be on sale. This factory generic ammunition using a 55-grain FMJ bullet is the best choice for plinking and practice.

Hornady's Steel Match is easily the finest steel cased rifle ammunition. The price is affordable.

The Federal American Eagle is up to practice and duty use, as far as that goes. A credible resource is the Black Hills Ammunition "blue box" remanufactured line. Reliable and affordable, the use of reprocessed cases is a big cost saver. I have avoided most steel cased ammunition, and not because it doesn't function. Foreign powder is often dirty and requires excess effort to scrub the bolt free of carbon deposits. Hornady's Steel Match is loaded by Hornady and performs as well as most Hornady loads, which is very good to excellent. I now use quite a bit of this load. The one that is found in bulk at a fair price is the one to choose. I have found that, if you are purchasing loads in bulk, boxer primed brass is longer lived in storage, versus the berdan-primed steel caseloads. Just in case, in an emergency situation a rifle may be loaded with quality practice ball ammunition and you can expect good reliability.

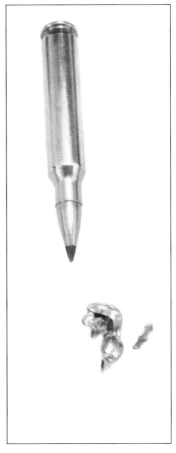

Most .223 loads are highly frangible.

Fiocchi's .300 Blackout practice load is affordable and accurate.

Competition

Competition means different things to different folks. Three-gun competition demands reliability, and the loads covered in the recreational section will work well. The National Match would be another thing. The long-range stages at 3-Gun demand more accuracy. I have used the Federal American Eagle 62-grain Tip at 300 yards. Available in a bulk box, this load would fill the bill at 3-Gun nicely. A number of competitors use the least expensive

Gorilla Ammunition has earned a good name with quality loads such as these .300 BAC loads.

possible 55-grain FMJ, then switch to something like the Black Hills Ammunition 60-grain JSP at longer range. Recently I obtained a number of the Fiocchi Canned Heat loads with the 62-grain FMJ bullet. You simply cannot criticize the packaging. The plastic lid is pulled away, and then there is another internal barrier similar to wax paper. Overall, a good kit for those who like to keep a ready supply in storage.

At long range, names such as Hornady and Sierra bullets dominate the field; the loads are filled with the individual's choice of IMR 4895 or Varget powder. Handloads not only keep cost down; they also allow the rifleman to fine tune the load. For the rest of us, beginning with the Black Hills Ammunition 52-grain MATCH, an old favorite, we have loads capable of cutting-edge accuracy. In heavier bullets, the 75-grain BTHP as loaded by High Precision Down Range (HPR) is never a bad choice. Long range demands precision. There are loads that are more accurate than I am able to hold. The

Gorilla Ammunition offers good quality, accurate, and reliable .223 loads.

Black Hills 77-grain OTM is the choice of the US Marine Corps and other units. Match the load to your rifle and control the trigger. These are excellent choices.

Varmints

The center fire .22 was conceived as a varmint round. We have managed to get much, much more from the cartridge than intended. Varmint hunting is a great pastime. The skill demanded crossovers into other fields. As an example, when my younger son graduated from basic training the best shot in the platoon was a young man from Montana who grew up shooting on the prairie. Accuracy is important, and so is a clean humane kill. Highly frangible bullets are the best choice. These bullets also limit ricochet and preserve public safety. Hornady's 36-grain NTX is both fast and accurate. I have also used the 40-grain V-Max, particularly in the Fiocchi load, and found it clean burning and accurate. Despite the shorter bearing surface, these loads have given excellent results on targets well past 200 yards. Another favorite is the Black Hills Varmint Grenade. On this subject, some years ago, a recommen-

dation was made that law officers and home defenders should use the 40-grain .223. Some bought into this, and the choice is a poor one for personal defense. These bullets are designed to blow up on a pest weighing a few ounces. The bullet would disintegrate on a belt buckle. The 55-grain JSP is plenty frangible for home defense! Both the 40-grain V-Max by Fiocchi and the Hornady 36-grain NTX function well in my Colt carbine, but they are varmint and pest loads, not service loads. That being said, they are excellent choices for the intended purpose.

Federal's Bonded Cores have earned an enviable reputation in both the game field and law enforcement.

Medium Game

A close friend has dropped a dozen deer in three seasons, with a single shot each using the .223 rifle. His Mini 14 was loaded in each case with the Winchester 69-grain JSP. This loading exhibits an excellent balance of expansion and penetration. It does not fragment, but mushrooms like a .30 caliber bullet. Some time ago I researched the .22 Savage High Power, a high-velocity number from a hundred years ago. The reason this caliber was not successful, most believe, was due to a lack of proper bullets for taking game. This is no longer true, and the .223 Remington can be a deer taker with proper bullets. The Winchester Ballistic Silvertip is another good load. These loads expand and hold their weight, rather than fragment. Another excellent choice is the Black Hills Ammunition load with the Barnes 55-grain

This is a 62-grain .223 from Federal Cartridge. As good as it gets!

TSX bullet. I have also tested the Black Hills Ammunition 62-grain TSX and find it an excellent all-around loading. They give the hunter every advantage. A superbly accurate choice is the Federal Vital Shock 60-grain JSP. This load uses the proven Nosler ballistic tip. Federal has recently introduced a 62-grain loading that is even more effective, per my testing, and match-grade accurate. The Trophy Bonded Vital Shock is a first-class loading with much to recommend.

Personal Defense

Personal defense isn't the same as military use or police service. Those who use the .223 for home defense must concentrate upon reliability and cartridge

PNW offers quality reliable loads that are well suited to use in the .300 Blackout.

integrity. The ready rifle or the magazine may be stored for use. (It is good to load the magazine down two in the twenty-round renditions and three in the thirty-round magazines; this releases more than 10 percent of the pressure on the spring.) Police shootings usually occur within 50 yards. Most are far shorter. The 55-grain JSP has been used across the board for many years. There are better choices, most of them intended to increase the penetration of the load and decrease fragmentation. As an example, some years ago an officer attempting to stop a fleeing robbery suspect fired a single 55-grain JSP into a vehicle windshield. The bullet fragmented in the glass and a portion of the bullet struck the felon. While the felon bled out, he did so after traveling some miles with a wound from a bullet fragment. Light cover penetration also needed to be enhanced. This is why special teams still rely upon the .308 precision rifle, in addition to the AR-15.

The .223 demonstrates less penetration in building materials and home structures than such common pistol calibers as the 9mm, .40, and .45. With standard loads beginning with the 55-grain JSP, results against felons in the open have been excellent, a single shot usually taking immediate effect. This is a good thing for public safety. In this regard, practically every .223 55-grain JSP is a good choice. After considerable research, I adopted the Black Hills Ammunition 60-grain JSP as my personal standard some time ago, and have seen little reason to change. The cartridge is available in fifty-round boxes with a "blue box" training round available. Another solution to the problem is the Hornady

A good rifle and the Innovativetargets.net steel gong can burn up a lot of ammunition!

60-grain A-Max loading. Available, affordable, and predictably effective, this loading is versatile and accurate. Winchester loads the Ballistic Silvertip in premium nickel-plated cases. I have explored the heavier bullets, particularly in light of the excellent results of the Black Hills Ammunition 77-grain OTM in the hands of our military marksmen. Heavy bullet loads are certainly formidable, but for my personal use I think the 60-grain loads are best. If my scenario included felons at 50–100 yards, I would reexamine the requirements. The cartridges and loads discussed are all top quality. I have tested each for reliability, accuracy, and ballistic performance. In the end, a loading that performs

Hornady's steel case SST load is among the most accurate loads in the 7.62×39mm rifle.

reliably in your personal rifle, and which exhibits good accuracy, is what's important. Consider the level of penetration needed and success is assured.

.308 WINCHESTER

The .308 is the heavy artillery of personal defense compared to the .223 Remington. While the .223 is effective inside of 100 yards if there are no intermediate barriers, the .223 falls short when greater penetration and range are needed. As a true all-around tactical marksman's rifle versus a dedicated squad marksman's rifle, the .308 has significant advantages. In a defensive situation, most shots will be to the torso. If there is a need to penetrate web gear and equipment carried on the chest, such as a carrier filled with ammunition, then the .308 comes out ahead of the .223 on every count. For this reason, shooters striving for top accuracy adopt the 168-grain MATCH loading. This is fine for accuracy and availability. However, this load and bullet combination doesn't offer better wound ballistics than FMJ loads. Law enforcement teams have adopted a number of loads that offer accuracy comparable or equal to the .308 MATCH with excellent terminal ballistics. These include the Hornady TAP and Hornady AMAX. Even if the Match King is more accurate, the AMAX is more than accurate enough, and offers an advantage in public safety and in terminal ballistics. The AMAX loads produce excellent wound ballistics in every test I have undertaken. The need for greater penetration than the .223 has been demonstrated by incidents in which the .223 did not provide adequate penetration in addressing vehicle

Hornady is a price leader in the top-end ammunition market. Fifty rounds of 7.62×39mm with the SST bullet is offered at a fair price.

Note picture-perfect expansion of the SIG SAUER .300 Blackout.

glass. In at least one incident, a .223 bullet shattered on a heavy plate glass and deflected during a rescue attempt. The Hornady AMAX has shown excellent penetration, followed by good wound potential after barrier penetration.

CHAPTER FIFTEEN

OTHER RIFLES

The most popular rifles in America are the AR-15 and the bolt-action .308 for critical use. But there are other rifles that are useful, and even superior in certain niches. The .223 rifle does not have to be an AR-15. There are some who like the classic handling of a wooden stock and semi-pistol grip. I obtained a Mini 14 as soon as possible after its introduction. I found the Mini-14 to be an excellent choice for personal defense, police work and predator culling. The Ruger is sometimes called a scaled-down M14. There is nothing wrong with that, but the Mini 14 is also a modern .30 carbine updated for the powerful .223 Remington cartridge. When it comes to accuracy, almost any AR-15 is more accurate than the Ruger Mini 14. The Mini 14 rifle is usually good for 2 inches at 50 yards with iron sights, but some are good for 3 inches at 100 yards, particularly the modern version when fitted with a proper rifle scope. The New York City Special Services District used the Ruger and enjoyed excellent results. The special unit's use of the M1 Carbine decades ago may have led to the adoption of the Ruger. A well-outfitted Mini-14 sets you back less than a comparable AR-15, although a cheap AR-15 may be less than the Ruger. Quality is not an issue—this is a Ruger, remember? The rifle always hit where I aimed it, and it popped a few predators and feral dogs along the way. The .223 was an emphatic stopper, and I do not recall needing a single follow-up shot. My friend, Roger, took twelve deer in a few years with his personal Ruger

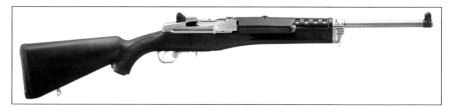

Ruger's Mini 14 is a useful rifle with friendly handling.

This synthetic stocked Mini 14 is a great all-around rifle. The stock will not warp in severe climatic conditions.

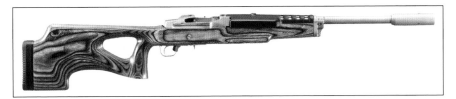

This is a pretty wild Ruger rifle, a great one for specialized use.

Mini-14 loaded with the Winchester 69-grain JSP. One shot each and the game was on the ground!

The Ruger handles brilliantly fast. AR ergonomics aside, try the Mini-14 sometimes because it is a revelation. For the chores for which you may really need a rifle, the Ruger shines. However, riflemen appreciate accuracy. When I took the time to benchrest the Ruger, I discovered my handy, light-kicking rifle was not that accurate at a long 100 yards. Even with the better grade of commercial ammunition, a 100-yard group of 3 inches was excellent, but 4 inches was more common. Bargain basement loads were worse. Some sought custom-grade barrels, and those did work well. A less expensive trick is simply relieving the stock around the gas block area, and in some cases relieving the gas block itself, stopping metal-on-metal friction. The result was shaving an inch off the total group size, sometimes more. With proper bedding and judicious gunsmithing, the Ruger became more useful. The point is, however, that straight out of the box the least accurate rifles were as accurate as the US M1 .30 carbine and far more powerful. Even the older guns would stay on a man-sized target at a long 100 yards. I am speaking of

The Ruger Ranch Rifle features excellent aperture sights.

previous generations of the Mini-14. The new rifle features a gas block redesign that alleviates much of the concerns with the old rifle. There were no reliability concerns and there are still none; however, accuracy is better. That upgrade occurred several years ago, and the Mini-14 over serial number prefix 580 has it. I am not eager to trade my long-serving Mini-14, even while admitting that the new product is a better rifle. That is as it should be. Some products are cheapened for ease of manufacture; Ruger has improved its machinery. You can count on the current rifle for three-shot, 100-yard groups of 2 inches with quality ammunition. The present incarnation gives you a good all-around accurate rifle. I tested the Fiocchi 69-grain JSP (Match-King) load in a new rifle with excellent results—one three-shot group went under 2 inches. When you consider how light and handy the rifle is, that is excellent performance. The rifle is 38 inches long and weighs 7 pounds. When all is said and done, the Ruger Mini-14 is a great all-around rifle. If I trust the rifle for police service, and the special units of NYPD do the same, it is probably going to do anything you need. My son, Alan, is the best shot I know, and he also likes the Mini-14. However, he prefers to load his own ammunition and the stainless-steel rifle. That is fine; either is a great choice. Expect to pay more for quality magazines compared to the AR-15 rifle.

Based on my experience with the AK-type rifle, I can say I have not been a fan. I have owned a few, usually due to an editorial assignment, not because it was something I wished to hang in the rack.

The AR-15 has been my rifle and I have spent my time mastering it. The AK seemed the rougher rifle, and that is its appeal to many. The AK-47 was designed for reliability and low maintenance. If you believe the AK never

This humble old AK has been treated to the camouflage treatment.

jams we are going to a different church, but the rifle is usually reliable. There have been any number of rather poor incarnations that simply do not live up to their promise. There are also a number of well-built and reliable rifles. The rifle covered in this review is one of these. I have strongly considered the AK-type of late as an answer to the need for a reliable but affordable rifle that most can use well. Post-Katrina musings aside, a reliable rifle is a good thing to have. The AK-47's origin came in street fighting at Stalingrad, and later Berlin, as the Russians pushed back the Germans and ultimately marched to Berlin. The Nagant rifle wasn't well suited to dynamic house clearing. The Soviet "burb gun" was a great close quarters weapon, but lacked the range and power of a rifle. The Soviets developed a short-range rifle cartridge with enough power to do the job, and with enough versatility to replace both the full-power rifle and the submachine gun. This is a simple description of a complex history, but the AK-47 was exactly what was needed. The Soviet narrative of the war was different from our own. The United States fought in North Africa and the mountains of Italy, where the Garand was a great rifle. The Soviets fought at long range as well, but the house-to-house fighting and rapid movement behind armor was also part of their war. By the time we were involved in Vietnam, the need for a jungle fighter produced the AR-15 rifle—and the rest is history.

Typical gas venting with 5.56mm AK.

As development of either rifle progressed, a steady goal has been to improve the accuracy of the type. The AR-15 is a wonderfully accurate rifle, and I do not think that reliability has been compromised in the best examples. For instance, my Colt HBAR, Colt SOCOM, and Daniel Defense have never malfunctioned, but then I have not marched in the sand box. The Israelis captured tens of thousands of AK rifles and ammunition, but seem disdainful about using them and favor the M16 types, although they built a home-grown AK variant. The Galil is a mix of AK features and the 5.56mm chambering. Sometimes conceptions are at variance with observations, and I wanted to test and evaluate one of the newest production AK variants to make up my own mind about the rifle. The Century International Arms PAP M90 caught my eye. This rifle is manufactured by Zastava Arms. I have enjoyed excellent results with their products in the past. The rifle seems well made of good material. The furniture is plastic. The forend and stock are a good fit. The stock, however, had an angle that worked on my cheek when I used the proper cheekweld. Since the recoil is light it was not going to jar my molars loose, but it was noticeable. My brother also fired the rifle and did not notice the angle on the stock. I adapted.

The rifle sports standard AK-type sights. The trigger action isn't overly heavy at 6.5 pounds, and is clean enough for decent work. Like most AK variants, the bolt does not lock open on the last shot. The bolt may be locked open with the safety. The safety is simply a lever on the side of the receiver. When applied, it locks the bolt shut. This safety was stiff at first, but worked in. Too loose leads to problems. The big news is that the rifle is chambered for the 5.56mm NATO cartridge. There have been 5.56mm AKs before, but they took specific magazines that were sometimes difficult to obtain. This Zastava features a hard plastic adaptor that accepts AR-15 magazines. AR magazines are cheap and plentiful. If you favor the 7.62×39mm cartridge, this isn't your rifle. If you like the simplicity and ruggedness of the AK, but like the easy availability of the AR magazine and ammunition, this is your rifle. I tested a number of both aluminum and polymer magazines, including the aluminum NHMTG, Colt, and OKAY, and the polymer Troy and Magpul. All worked well without any problems. This is interesting, since the much more expensive Beretta ARX did not accept all AR-15 magazines. The Beretta ARX uses a gas piston instead of the direct impingement of the AR-15, and all AK types also used the gas piston. There is enough give in this system to allow the AK to function with a bit of dirt in the action, or with less than perfect ammunition. No surprises there.

The sights of the AK-type rifle are rugged and useful. It was not difficult to adjust them for combat range, 25 yards, and also to adjust the sight for elevation at a long 100 yards. While the receiver features a device for mounting an optic, I think that most of us will be better served with iron sights. The AK is a rugged "go anywhere, do anything" rifle; and while accuracy potential is increased by a quality optic, the rifle is useful as issued. I fired the rifle with over two hundred rounds at the first range outing. This is an enjoyable rifle to fire and use. Allowing the rifle to cool in between loading magazines, there were no failures to feed, chamber, fire, or eject. I began firing with Winchester's USA 55-grain FMJ loading. I fired quickly, firing offhand, and engaging targets quickly. Cases are ejected smartly. However, it wasn't long before the receiver picked up the characteristic

When using the PTR 91, be certain the magazine is properly seated.

brass mark from cases hitting the receiver. It would not be an AK without this. I also fired a full box of Hornady's Steel Match loads. This is about the most affordable quality load available. I did not expect an AK to have any problem with steel caseloads. During this firing program, I practiced quickly changing magazines. The push button magazine release works fine. The limiting factor is that the bolt doesn't hold open on the last shot. The rifle isn't as fast to reload as an AR, but is superior to the original AK system.

I also fired a number of loads that are not something the AK was intended for. Fiocchi's 40-grain V-Max is a blistering fast number intended to vaporize varmints at long range. At 3,600 fps, this is a great load. Part of the reason the AK is so reliable is that the over-the-barrel gas piston has a bit of tolerance for different loads. In any case, this load ran right through a magazine without complaint. I blasted dirt clods and clay birds at the 100-yard line with good results. Next up came a heavy weight. Fiocchi offers a 69-grain load that is gilt-edged accurate in the right rifle. This one breaks about 2,700 fps. The results were good with twenty rounds through the PMAG in no time, and with good accuracy in informal shooting. Absolute accuracy was tested by firing at 100 yards. With iron sights this type of shooting is as much about

muscle control and a good firing position as it is about sight alignment and sight picture, but it is all important. I fired the Winchester USA 55-grain FMJ, Hornady 55-grain Steel Match, and Fiocchi 69-grain Extrema, firing five-shot groups. The rifle, surprisingly, fired to the same point of aim

The PTR 91 rifle sights are the best of the breed, and that includes the original HK 91.

more or less with all three loads. Accuracy was consistent, with most groups just under 4 inches. I managed one 3-inch and one 0.5-inch group. This is better than most 7.62×39mm rifles. I bumped and adjusted the sights, and was able to get good results in offhand fire as well. The bottom line: this is a shooter. It is accurate enough, reliable, and clearly a good-to-go rifle for alarms and excursions.

The PTR 91 company was originally formed in order to give American shooters an affordable version of the HK 91 rifle. The JLD company purchased arms-making equipment including gauges, machinery, engineering drawings, and diagrams needed to produce a direct copy of the HK 91. They improved the theme to produce a more accurate rifle. Today the PTR 91 rifles are made in a modern manufacturing plant on CNC machinery. The operation of the rifle isn't gas or recoil operated in the conventional sense. The rifle employs a delayed blowback system with a non-rotating head and twin rollers. These rollers, located on the bolt on each side, lock into detents in the trunnion of a stamped steel receiver. On firing, force on the bolt keeps the action locked until the bullet exits the barrel; then the action unlocks and the bolt is jolted to the rear against spring pressure. The bolt then returns to battery, stripping a cartridge from the magazine along the way. The PTR 91 and the Century C 308 use the characteristic fluted chamber that helps to dispel pressure and allow easier extraction of the fired case. There is an interesting history behind these rifles, beginning with engineers escaping Germany after World War II and developing the Spanish CETME rifle, followed by the adoption of the rifle by Germany as the G 3/HK 91. We must mention that PTR Inc. recently moved from Connecticut to South Carolina, largely due to an unfavorable legislative session passing draconian gun laws. The owner noted that it is practically impossible for any business, let alone a gun maker, to deal with the government in his home state. A somewhat difficult situation was resolved by moving to a free state.

The PTR 91 rifle is based upon the HK 91. The GI version as tested represents a base rifle. There are elevated rifles, tactical rifles, and target guns available from PTR 91, but they share the same action. A class of .308 battle rifles similar to the FN FAL, the original HK 91, and G3 rifles are in use worldwide. The operation of the rifle is straightforward. An operating handle on the left side of the barrel is used to cock the action. This handle does not reciprocate with the bolt as the rifle fires. The cocking handle may be used to lock the rifle open. The barrel features a six-ported muzzle brake. The synthetic forend offers excellent gripping surface. Just below the cocking handle is a checkered section about 4.25 inches long. The ribbed, vented forend offers good adhesion when the rifle is fired. The firing grip handle isn't stippled, but it is smooth and hollow. The handle offers good retention by its geometry. The receiver is particularly well finished. The bolt is also well polished. The welds necessary on a stamped steel receiver are less pronounced and noticeable than other HK 91 clones. The magazine release is tight and positive in operation. The safety operates smoothly with a positive indent. All of the controls are readily accessible and allow rapid manipulation. Trigger compression is smooth, but is relatively heavy at 9.5 pounds. The stock features a hard rubber recoil pad. I like the muzzle brake of the GI Model, and in firing it seems to have made a difference in control. The PTR 91 features a shrouded front post sight. The rear diopter sight is among the best battle sights ever fielded, in my opinion. The drum is easily moved from the 100-meter position to the 400-meter position. The short-range setting uses an open V-type rear sight. The others use an aperture rear sight. The PTR 91 uses a company-developed rear sight that also features a windage adjustment. This is an important advantage in a rifle intended for all-around use.

There are a number of different magazines in existence for the CETME, C91, and HK 91 .308 rifles. I tested a total of twelve magazines with my personal rifle. All locked in the PTR without difficulty. However, I have not enjoyed this compatibility with the C91 and C308 rifles. In the first C91 rifle four locked as designed, but four gave trouble and required a hard slap to properly seat. In the third rifle, purchased used at the pawn shop and thus not given as much credibility as the new C91, only four of the magazines would lock. While enthusiasts are aware of the situation, this is a point in favor of the PTR 91. Prior to firing the rifle, be certain your rifle is well lubricated. Since PTR recommends a one-hundred-round break-in period, I used five magazines my first go-around, loaded with twenty rounds each of the Winchester 147-grain FMJ in one magazine, the Fiocchi 150-grain FMJ load in one magazine, and Portuguese surplus in the other magazines. Do not let initial failures to fully close the bolt on firing worry you. The PTR 91 is a tight rifle, and the roller cam action must be worked in. During my work with several of these rifles it has not been unusual to have failures to lock the bolt in firing the first magazine, and an occasional failure up to the fourth magazine, but after the first hundred cartridges the rifle should be good to go. Do not use heavy weight bullets over 168 grains, and do not use handloads in the break-in period. Either Winchester or Fiocchi ball should be used so as not to cloud the reliability issue.

As for absolute accuracy, there are several models of the PTR 91 rifle and they differ in basic accuracy. With good quality ammunition, 1.5–2.0 MOA is expected. Using the Black Hills 168-grain MATCH load, I have fired a number of groups as small as three shots into 1.25 inches. This demands great concentration and perfect muscular control, a sharp eye on the sights, and perfect trigger control. As such, these 1.25-inch groupings for three shots at 100 yards are not the norm, but they occur often enough to underwrite the rifle's intrinsic accuracy.

The Century C91 operates in the same manner as the PTR rifle. The major difference is the fit and finish, with the PTR having a green tint in the GI gun and a deeper finish in all models. The C91 and C308 rifles exhibit more weld marks. The trigger action of the C91 I tested most extensively was a heavy 10.5 pounds. It has not proven as accurate as the PTR 91 rifle. The single best group I have fired with the C91-type rifle has been 1.5 inches with the Silver State Armory 168-grain loading. The average is closer to 2.5 inches, and some 3-inch groups with FMJ generic loads. A great improvement was realized when I fitted a PRS2 stock from Magpul Industries. This rifle stock allows length of pull adjustment from about 15 to 16.2 inches. The cheek piece allows changes up to 1.8 inches, and fore and after adjustment of 0.65 inch. The C91 class of rifle has a forward weight bias, and the heavier than standard stock results in an excellent feel. With this addition, the rifle felt much better in any firing position, relieving a complaint concerning the stocks found on the rifles. This part will fit either the PTR or the C91 rifles. This rifle was purchased used; it proved more finicky concerning magazine fit than the first, but with a properly fit magazine proved equally reliable. However, neither the C91 nor the C308 marked rifles required a break-in period. I think that the PTR 91 is the better rifle, but the Century is worth the price.

Ruger's Scout Rifle is a formidable all-around bolt-action rifle. It doesn't get any better than an affordable Scout.

THE RUGER SCOUT RIFLE

Some years ago, Jeff Cooper formulated a base line for the firearm he called the Scout Rifle. The rifle would have a good optic, but not necessarily a high-power optical sight. The rifle would be short, light for the caliber, and would fire the .308 Winchester cartridge. It would incorporate a rugged bolt-action design and be fitted with a top-flight sling. Cooper envisioned the rifle as a game getter, but also as a viable rifle for alarms and excursions in the United States and abroad. The concept took root, with Steyr manufacturing a close approximation of the Scout idea. Among the more useful and effective of modern Scout rifles is the M77 variant offered by Ruger firearms. This rifle is affordable and, like all Ruger bolt-action rifles, reliable. The M77 features a controlled feed action. The difference between controlled feed and push feed is important. With the Mauser 98 type action, the extractor is in control of the cartridge throughout its travel. The bolt is racked to the rear. As the cartridge rises in the magazine, the cartridge case rim is pushed under the extractor. The extractor firmly grasps the cartridge rim. The cartridge is chambered. After firing, the claw extractor takes a solid bite on the cartridge rim and extracts the spent cartridge. With the push feed design, the extractor does not control the cartridge. The cartridge is pushed into the chamber. After firing, the force of extraction is less than with the controlled feed rifle design. Push feed designs, such as in the Remington 700, seldom give trouble. Nevertheless, in a worst-case scenario the controlled feed is the superior action. Certainly, for dangerous game or critical

The Ruger's aperture sights are first class. Note Picatinny rail for optics.

You can never go wrong with a synthetic stock on a proper Scout rifle!

use the controlled feed should be chosen. When you are firing from a less than perfect firing position, or are slanted in any way, the push feed action is less positive in feeding. When you have the option of controlled feed action you should choose it.

With its controlled feed, Mauser extractor, and three-position safety, the Ruger Scout Rifle is a great all-around rifle. The rifle features a ten-round detachable box magazine. The newest rifles sport excellent triggers. The Ruger receiver features a flat bottom. Within recent memory, a large amount of cash was spent altering actions to the flat bottom that Ruger now offers as a matter of course. This rifle also features an angled bedding screw attached to the receiver's recoil lug. There are good mounts for Ruger rings and bases, and excellent fixed sights supplied with the rifle. It features a 16.5-inch barrel. At present the rifle is available in both .223 Remington and .308 Winchester. I fail to see the appeal of the .223 chambering compared to the .308 in this particular rifle. The sights are similar to the Mini 14 rifle. A Picatinny rail offers plenty of options. The flash suppressor brings the rifle's barrel length to 19 inches. I am not certain we need this flash suppressor on a bolt-action rifle, but the .308 is more pleasant to fire with this type of device. I can notice a difference between this rifle's recoil and my personal short-barrel Remington 700. The Remington isn't unpleasant to fire; it's just that the Ruger is simply more comfortable. The flash suppressor is removable, if you prefer. The stock is well designed and fits most shooting styles. The recoil pad is a full one-inch thick, and there are spacers supplied with the rifle that allow adjustment of some two inches. This means the rifle is quite versatile and can be adjusted for a wide variety of shooters. The magazine well and the trigger guard are plastic, or, as it is called, fiberglass impregnated nylon. The magazine release is similar to the Mini 14 and works well in practice. The location just ahead of the trigger guard works for rapid changes. The magazine holds ten cartridges and is not difficult to load. The manual of arms requires the cartridge to be forced down against the follower, and then to the rear. They cannot be pressed directly from above. This allows the same feed cycle as when the Mauser-type bolt feeds from a fixed magazine. The feel during feeding is different from a push feed, but similar to a Mauser 98 rifle.

The rifle is a very good one, and is a good example of Cooper's Scout rifle. Of course, there are always some who say that the rifle isn't quite what Cooper envisioned; but then, what is? I am not an engineer, but can draw a pretty mean tic-tac-toe diagram, so I leave design to the masters at Ruger. The rifle may be brought into standard if you disagree, but the Ruger Scout Rifle is a very capable rifle. It is true that the magazine cannot be topped off from the top. It is heavier than the original Scout concept, but then perhaps most shooters would feel that a lighter rifle kicks too much. It all depends on whether you call Cooper's work a strict edict or a guideline. I like the rifle very much as it is. The Ruger was intended to be good for about 2 inches for a three-shot group at 100 yards. Today, manufacturing tolerances and quality ammunition make for a higher standard than in Colonel Cooper's day. Remarkably affordable rifles will shoot good groups with factory ammunition. The need for the 1-inch group is among the hardiest of perennials. For field use this isn't necessary. The Ruger Scout Rifle, however, is an accurate rifle. The action is smooth and always works. Feed is smooth. I was able to fire for accuracy at both 50 yards and 100 yards. I used the Winchester 147-grain USA FMJ to get sighted and Winchester 168-grain MATCH for record. At 50 yards with open sights, 2 inches on demand turned into 1.5 inches at my best. At a long 100 yards, using every technique to my advantage, the iron sights gave a credible 2.5 inches with the 168-grain MATCH load. Things would have gone more quickly, and doubtless with greater accuracy, with a good rifle scope. The Scout Rifle is intended as a "go anywhere, do anything rifle"—a rifle for those who have only one rifle. Think about it this way: During an emergency, you will have only one rifle, the one on your back. The Scout rifle is a good choice.

An interesting variation on the theme is the Ruger M77 Dangerous Game Rifle. I have no personal experience with this Ruger, but have fired a pre-64 Winchester .375 H and H extensively. A reliable and affordable bolt-action rifle chambered for .375 or .416 cartridges might be the ideal survival gun for those in the wilds of Alaska. There are animals that regard man as a nuisance, and that are not easily dissuaded by lighter rifles. These are great rifles, well worth their price.

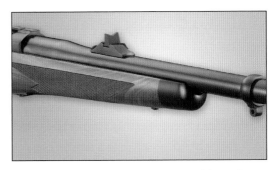

The Ruger Alaskan rifle features express sights and excellent hand fitting.

This is a heavy-duty Ruger rifle in .375 Magnum. Few of us will need this rifle.

THE LONG-ACTION LEVER-ACTION GUNS

The long-action lever-action rifles include the Savage 99 rifle and the Winchester 1895 rifle. Although each is a classic and the Winchester is still in production, their overall utility is limited. The originals are too valuable for use as an all-around tactical "go anywhere, do anything rifle." In addition, they are too old to be completely trusted. The lever-action throw is longer than the .30-30 rifle, since the action is longer to account for the .300 Savage, .30-40, and other cartridges for which these rifles are chambered. These rifles are great hunting rifles for the person who prefers them, and I certainly admire the design and history of these firearms. But for modern, practical use, there are much better choices.

THE .30 CARBINE

The .30 M1 Carbine is a rifle that simply will not die. I have fired a dozen examples during the past decade. They are light, handy, fast handling, and make for a superior CQB rifle for the home. I would rather have a .30 caliber carbine than any modern 5.7mm PDW firearm. In some situations, such as for home defense, the carbine might be superior to the AR-15 based on handiness and light weight. Expense, recoil, and muzzle blast are less with the .30 carbine. The bottom line, as always, is that the rifle must be completely reliable. You must fire the example, in order to be certain. Fifteen-round magazines usually work well. The thirty-round magazines are less reliable. The modern Auto-Ordnance carbine is, in my estimation, the best of the .30 carbine clones. Accuracy isn't the long suit of the .30 carbine, but then consider its mission. Most of the Auto-Ordnance carbines will group three shots of the Hornady JSP into 4 inches at 100 yards. GI carbines may be improved with careful bedding, but it is what it is. The .30 carbine is a specialized firearm primarily useful for home defense. In that role, it is superior to the most expensive tactical handgun. It is limited for the purpose of hunting and outdoor uses. While capable of taking predators and pests at moderate range, this isn't a deer cartridge.

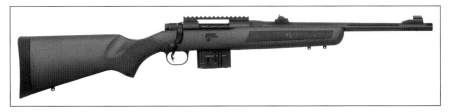

The Thunder Ranch Mossberg patrol rifle adds a bit of flair to the Scout rifle concept.

BUDGET BOLT-ACTION RIFLES

For the rifleman primarily interested in hunting, there are a number of inexpensive but useful bolt-action rifles. These include the Mossberg ATR, Ruger American, and the Savage Axis. Some are offered in a package with an affordable rifle scope. I have fired most and find them worth the money— and some are worth a little more. A lot of

The author finds the Mossberg .223 MVP rifle a great all-around light rifle.

research and development has gone into the entry level rifle. The price point isn't everything, and some of the engineering that went into these rifles is impressive. They are a cut above the once popular trade store rifles. The modern bolt-action rifle with a synthetic stock and affordable price tag is important. With this rifle, you can purchase a good .22, a decent AR-15, plus a high-powered hunting rifle, and not break the bank. Let's face it, much of the interest in shooting will hinge upon access and entry cost. Family hunts are given more opportunity by using an affordable rifle. In the past, store brands such as Revelation and Ted Williams offered good value. Today, the Savage Axis and Mossberg ATR offer much the same value, but they are significantly better rifles. There have been false starts and recalls—the Remington 710 was one—and the modern Savage Axis seems, if not the best buy, then among the best buys on the market. I have observed excellent accuracy from the Savage Axis rifle, which in my experience isn't out of the norm. At the Axis price point, you can afford a good scope and plenty of practice ammunition. Let's examine the Savage as a typical affordable rifle.

When handling the Savage rifle, the ejection port is generous, offering plenty of room for loading and unloading cartridges. The stock fits the action. I think that the wrist is a bit thin, but handling is good, and the rifle—a .30-06

The Savage Axis/Vanguard optics combination has proven a good one.

example—was never uncomfortable to fire. These rifles feature a detachable box magazine, a feature modern shooters seem to prefer. The Mossberg ATR, as an example, uses the blind box magazine. The stock and integral locking lugs of the Savage rifle get good marks. The stock isn't ugly and the molding is adequate; it is, after all, a modern black stock. I fitted a Vanguard scope to the rifle and tightened every nut and bolt down before range work. The Vanguard scope is clear with excellent adjustments, and leaves nothing to be desired in a hunting scope. The rifle comes to the shoulder quickly, balances well, and isn't a burden during a long day in the field. I benchrested the rifle with the 155-grain A-Max load from Black Hills ammunition first, and I have also used the 168-grain A-Max loading. The results were excellent by any standard. The average of the first three-shot groups with the 155-grain load was 1.25 inches. The 168-grain load inched into just less than an inch. I fired six rounds of the Nosler 180-grain InterBond loading from the rifle. This Black Hills load is for heavy game and offers excellent penetration. In some ways, this load maximizes the .30-06 Springfield cartridge. Recoil was there; so was accuracy. This load broke an exceptional 0.9 inch for the average of two groups. At this point I could easily see how a shooter might sight the rifle in and retire the piece until hunting season. Just the same, offhand work and firing from field positions demands practice. I have worked up a practice load that is sensibly below factory standards with the Sierra 150-grain JSP and enough 4064 for 2,600 fps. The Savage Axis/Vanguard combination is my go-to hunting rifle.

MOSSBERG ATR

When purchasing a rifle, our expectations often tie to the amount of cash we spend. In this case, we get a reliable and accurate rifle without the finish and high-grade stock of a more expensive firearm. Just the same, there is pride of ownership in a rifle that performs as well as this one. Modern CNC machining results in precise tolerances. If I am taking a rifle hunting, I am not certain I want to knock about the woods with an expensive rifle. I need one that works and is effective. My personal ATR is chambered for my favorite rifle caliber, the .308 Winchester. I sighted the rifle with its Simmons scope, and Winchester .308 USA load in 147-grain FMJ flavor. These FMJ loads are inexpensive and offer good accuracy. Using the box method, I quickly sighted in the rifle and then enjoyed firing it so much that I used another twenty-round box on clay birds and the like at 100 yards. The rifle handles quickly; the trigger press is fast and crisp, and the bolt is smooth with a short throw. There really is nothing to dislike about this rifle. This particular ATR is a short action, which simply means my rifle is chambered for a relatively short cartridge, the .308 Winchester. The .243 is also a short action. The .270 Winchester and .30-06 are long-action rifles. The receiver is long to accommodate longer cartridges. The short-action rifle has a short travel, or throw, easy to handle and fast in action. It features a blind-box magazine. The safety is handy and positive on the right side of the receiver, a location that does not interfere with scope mounting. The 18-inch barrel is light, and the rifle handles quickly. The last third or so of the barrel is fluted. I like that touch, and while practical advantage may be slight the look is great. Weight is reduced and, theoretically, heat is dissipated in a long firing session. The stock is what I call a "sporter" style. There is checkering on the pistol grip and forend that should keep your hand stabilized even if it is cold or sweaty. The stock design helps the eye line up quickly and naturally with the scope's objective lens. The rifle stock wears an effective butt pad. If you desire, the butt pad features a section you can remove to convert the ATR to a youth model. Firing off the benchrest, accuracy was credible. With the Winchester "White Box" loading, average two-shot groups at 100 yards were in the 2-inch range. Switching to the Winchester 168-grain MATCH load, these groups were on the order of 1.5 inches with the single best of three groups a scant 1.25 inches. The Winchester Ballistic Silvertip, a credible hunting load, was accurate at the football field range and will be the standard hunting load. The short ATR is a neat rifle well worth its price.

I would be remiss to leave out the .270 Winchester. While the .308 is a great all-around cartridge worthy of being emphasized in this book, the .30-06 is clearly the more powerful cartridge. The need for a long-action rifle makes for a heavier weight, but the power increase is notable. The .270 Winchester is also a powerful cartridge, but it is intended for long-range performance on thin-skinned game. This is a long-range elk rifle. The .30-06 would be more useful for bears. The .270 Winchester is among the most versatile and effective cartridges in America. The .270 was introduced in 1925 and has proved popular ever since. The .270 is simply a .30-06 Springfield necked down to .277 caliber. It is intended for long-range work and killing power at moderate range. The cartridge is accurate and effective, but doesn't kick as hard as some rifle cartridges. The .270 has taken every species of North American game. While perhaps light for the largest bears, the cartridge stands alone for versatility. As an example, the 90-grain bullet may be loaded to 3,600 fps. This makes the .270 an effective varmint cartridge. Sure, we will probably use a .223, but for the man with one rifle the .270 is a varmint buster. A 100-grain bullet at 3,500 fps is another option. The enthusiastic handloader can make the .270 talk! The standard 130-grain bullet at 3,100 fps is a good all-around

Ruger's takedown rifle is an excellent one for any crisis.

deer load for long range. There is also a 150-grain bullet for heavier game. The .270 is efficient with a variety of loads and bullet weights. The accuracy of the cartridge is demonstrated off the benchrest, while ballistic media demonstrates the power of the cartridge. The balance of penetration and controlled expansion of these loads is excellent. I particularly like the .270's neck design. There is plenty of tension in the neck with all bullet weights, even with the lightest bullets. While lighter and faster bullets may be used, the standard 130-grain load shoots flat over long distances. While some may master magnum cartridges, I do not own a magnum rifle. I prefer the .308, .270, and .30-06 cartridges. They do the business with accuracy, efficiency, and less bruising and raising of eddies in the skin. The cartridge responds well to a careful handloader. Effect on game is reliable.

My experiments with the Mossberg ATR/.270 rifle combination have been good. What really counts, and the reason I was led to this combination, are the glowing reports of the .270's effect in the field. This is why the .270 has been called the rifleman's rifle. Nothing I have observed can contradict this statement. I fitted a Vanguard Endeavor RS 41240 BDC riflescope to my personal rifle in an effort to give myself an edge in the field. (The same example used on the Savage Axis rifle.) This scope features good adjustment, clear optics, and good zero retention. Adjustment was rapid. It was with a minimum expenditure of ammunition that the rifle was sighted in. When choosing rifle ammo for the .270, the field is broad. Hornady offers at least nine loads from 100 to 150 grains. The Sierra 90-grain Varmint bullet is a handloading proposition, and Hornady bullets are available as components. As I often do, I searched for an economical loading to get the hang of the rifle and to sight it in. During the initial evaluation, I used the Fiocchi 130-grain JSP, and later fired the Fiocchi 150-grain loads. Accuracy was good and the powder burn was clean. While testing, I learned two things. The .270 kicks more than the .308, but then it is a larger cartridge. It also burns more powder and churns up a bit more horsepower. But it kicks less than a comparable .30-06 rifle. In addition, the .270 and the Mossberg ATR were accurate for a bargain rifle with a great scope, but not quite as accurate as the Savage Axis. Not surprising. Considering that it takes an excellent rifleman to stand on his legs and fire a three-shot 5-inch group at 100 yards, I think the .270 offers all of the accuracy I need. Using premium Black Hills Gold loads, the rifle will cut a three-shot group of 1.25 inches, with most loads about 1.5 inches. The rifle is sighted to strike 2 inches high at 100 yards, which gives me a dead-on hold to 200 yards. If you cannot shoot, of course, you may as well throw rocks. However, that is the accuracy this rifle and cartridge are capable of delivering. One thing is for certain—if I get a shot and do not connect with the game, it isn't the fault of the gun or the ammo. It is mine alone. This rifle is a credible choice for anyone on any budget. As you can see from the details of performance, these inexpensive bolt-action rifles deliver the goods. The primary focus of this book is to outfit the shooter with reliable gear that he can afford and use well. These rifles fit well in that niche.

I am often asked which bolt-action rifle is the best, regardless of price, and this is not usually fielded from a competition shooter, but from a person looking for a hunting rifle. The American-made rifles, the Japanese Howa, and the Austrian Steyr are all good rifles. The handling of one or the other may appeal to any given shooter. Some will find the more modern rifles suit them better than traditional blue steel and walnut rifles. One of the aspects that deserves attention is the locking lug design. We have discussed controlled feed versus push feed, and I have pointed out that controlled feed is best when you can have it. Locking lugs are also worth a study. Almost all bolt-action rifles designed prior to 2000 have two locking lugs. The Browning A bolt has three lugs. Remember this: two opposing lugs make for a 90-degree lift, while three lugs (Ruger American) make for a shorter 60-degree lift. The 60-degree bolt lift has a shorter arc, so you may find it faster in operation. The rifles open easily with the 60-degree lift and seem as strong as any design. If you examine the bolt body itself, you will find that the great majority of bolt bodies measure .690 on a micrometer. That is pretty uniform, and a good argument that one is as strong as the other. Then there are those who state that perhaps both bolts do not lock as tightly as we would like. This is very difficult to gauge. When a rifle does not show excess pressure signs with my top end handloads, and seems very accurate, my assumption is that the bolt lugs are locking tightly.

MOSSBERG MVP

The Mossberg MVP is a light bolt-action rifle with a fluted barrel, flat bottom forend, smooth bolt action, and a generous magazine capacity. It is designed as a sporting rifle for popping varmints, crows, predators, and other types of small game. It is related to the Mossberg Patrol rifle, a similar bolt-action rifle designed for law enforcement use. The MVP isn't supplied with iron sights, but with a Weaver-type rail for mounting an optic. This rifle has several advantages. First, it is affordable; second, it looks good; and third, it is more accurate than one might first suppose. Another advantage is that this rifle accepts AR-15-type magazines. The MVP Varmint rifle is quite interesting in its particulars. The bolt is fluted, which once was a custom touch. The bolt handle is swept back for rapid manipulation, and the trigger is a modern user adjustable type. The rifle is based upon modern design principles and chambered for the 5.56mm NATO cartridge. The rifle was designed from the beginning for use with AR-15 magazines, which took some effort. There are many 5.56mm bolt guns, but not many that use a removable magazine. The bolt had to be modified to feed from a box magazine, rather

The MVP rifle features good accuracy and is affordable. It handles well offhand.

than from a blind magazine. There is a small lever at about six o'clock on the bolt face. This lever acts as a feed guide to grab a cartridge from the magazine. The lever has a little give in its motion, and when the round is chambered this lever moves to fit close to the bolt face. I hope it works well in the long term. I purposely slammed the bolt hard on a couple of magazines. This is abuse, but you will probably slam the bolt pretty hard during a critical incident. It works just fine. These days, major companies tend not to let something out the door without major trial and error. The bolt itself is pretty interesting. The fluted bolt is attractive. Take care during disassembly. It isn't that tricky, but it is different than most two lug bolts. The extractor demands care due to its strong extractor spring. The ability to use an AR-15 magazine is good, especially if you own an AR-15 as well as this rifle.

However, some effort is needed in choosing magazines. The AR-15 features a magazine well that encompasses much of the magazine and keeps it steady. The Mossberg does not. The magazines will rattle. Ten-round magazines are less offensive, and some of the polymer magazines are a tighter fit. The magazine release works well. All in all, a good system and one that makes for good utility. If you live in one of the "People's Republics" that limit semiautomatic rifle ownership, this is the rifle for you.

This is the interesting MVP bolt. Note lever for feeding from an AR-15 magazine.

The stock is nicely checkered. The feel is good, the wood to metal fit excellent, and overall I find it a useful and nice looking stock. The trigger is called the LBA, or Lightning Bolt Action; it is adjustable for a lighter let-off. If reserved for personal defense and general pest and predator popping at moderate ranges, I think that the 3.5 pounds at which the rifle came set would be more than adequate. However, if you are going to set on a hill and address a varmint population at 200 yards or more, then setting the trigger for 2.5 pounds would be advisable. Trigger adjustment is easy enough. Take the rifle down and look to the trigger action. There is a screw in front of the trigger action; simply turn this slotted screw. This trigger and the rifle's overall quality and good fit are part of the reason the rifle is so accurate. The barrel is short but stiff and fluted toward the muzzle. The barrel lug features a tight fit to the stock. The barrel is stamped one in nine twist. The barrel twist is important in a .223 rifle, but then this is a 5.56mm rifle. While it is a thrice-told tale, the .223 Remington and the 5.56mm NATO are not quite the same. With the NATO chamber, this rifle will be able to safely use surplus ammunition without any danger.

The rifle is well balanced and looks good when properly set up. The Mossberg is lighter than my .308 and heavier rifles, and so took some acclimation. Accuracy limitations are going to be more about the shooter. Getting the butt into the shoulder, grasping the forearm correctly, and controlling the trigger is what counts with this rifle. Recoil is light, hardly a consideration. There is no muzzle brake as is the case with the Patrol Rifle, and that is something I can do without. The rifle proved quite accurate on the range. I have seen rifles that were dogs and did not improve, and rifles that were superbly accurate from the beginning. The Mossberg MVP is the most accurate rifle in the weight class I have fired. This means that you have to pay attention to detail. This isn't a benchrest rifle, but one that will serve well in the field. I fitted a Nikko Sterling, an inexpensive scope that worked okay in this application. The first load I tested was the affordable American Eagle 50-grain JHP. I used this load to get the rifle sighted in and to get the initial "feel" for the MVP. Results were good, with a three-shot group of 1.5 inches at 100 yards. Since this is a varmint rifle, I tried the Federal 40-grain Nosler Ballistic Tip. This is a great choice for vaporizing varmints, with typical Federal quality control. Results were excellent, with a 0.8-inch three-shot group at 100 yards. I wanted to try at least one heavier bullet, so I loaded the 62-grain Fusion. This number put three bullets into 0.9 inch. I was not cleaning the barrel nor letting it cool between shots. The .223/5.56mm rifle is regarded as an accurate combination, but this rifle is a tack driver and accuracy comes easily to a practiced shooter. I like this rifle a lot. It is my number one choice for introducing shooters to the centerfire rifle. For most of what I need, a rifle like this serves my purposes.

SAFETY OPERATION AND LOCATION

Some rifles feature simple safety levers on the right side of the receiver. Forward is fire, and to the rear is safe. Some lock the bolt when on safe, some do not. Some shooters like the ability to work the bolt and load the rifle with the safety on. The Mauser three-position safety is still a great option. The safety positions are fire, safety on bolt unlocked, and safety on bolt locked. Spend some time handling each type before you buy. For some, the safety location is more important than bolt lift. Another consideration is the trigger action. Most of us are served with a clean, crisp trigger of four pounds or so in a bolt-action rifle. An experienced rifleman may come to prefer a trigger action of three pounds or slightly less. Let experience be your guide. If you think that you may be interested in adjusting the trigger until you find a sweet spot, then by all means purchase a Savage rifle equipped with the Accu-Trigger, or a new Remington 700 with adjustable trigger.

I have not mentioned several of the popular calibers. I am well aware of the good properties of the .243 Winchester, and the excellent efficiency of the 7mm-08. For the beginner and the practical shooter on a budget, the calibers mentioned are good choices. For some it will be the caliber they cling to throughout their shooting life; for others, only a beginning.

CHAPTER SIXTEEN

ACCESSORIES AND MAGAZINES

T he Black Rifle is America's rifle. A bulwark against terrorists and criminals, a competition rifle and a hunting rifle, the original Armalite design has become an American icon. Like many instruments, the AR-15 is most useful in trained hands. Of course, anyone who owns a rifle purely for pride of ownership yet seldom fires it is exercising an important right.

This magazine carrier from Brownells has given yeomen service in testing many rifles.

But I believe that those who fire the rifle often and master the type are living the better dream! When I look over the handful of AR-15 rifles in my family, I sometimes ponder that old question: If I could have only one rifle, which would it be? And, when traveling, that is a question that must be answered. I do not take one on each shoulder when hunting. I want a credible tactical rifle and not a Rooney gun with too much gear hanging on the rail. While the rifle is a reliable design, I wish to seek out modifications that make the rifle more reliable but add nothing that will impede function. Some additions have distinct advantages, others do not. The added weight must be considered. Walking twenty feet to the benchrest isn't a problem, but carrying the rifle all day could be. Recoil isn't a problem with the AR-15, but muzzle blast can be when in confined quarters. And some of us like the .308 caliber AR-15. The LANTAC Dragon muzzle brake goes a long way in calming down the big bore AR rifle. A consistent trigger is more important than a light trigger, but as time goes on I find myself favoring match-grade triggers in the AR-15 rifle. And so it goes with a personal rifle.

THE INDIVIDUAL RIFLE

Service rifles are issued with strict rules on modification. A write-up or the stockade are likely results of playing with an issued rifle. As the man said, "There are many like it, but this one is mine." By carefully choosing additions to your personal rifle, you will be able to form a more personal bond with it. When knocking down steel targets at 200 yards, or facing a takeover home invasion, this bond is vital. Soldiers drill in order to be completely familiar with their rifles. You need to get to the range and fire the rifle often, clean and disassemble the rifle, and get with the program. Once you have fired one thousand rounds or so in a rifle, you will have bonded with it and understand your needs more closely. Some of the proposed modifications will be ergonomic; others will be related to sighting equipment. When you become hooked on shooting the AR-15, modifications to the bolt carrier and trigger system may be profitable. An NP3 coated bolt carrier makes function smoother, and also makes cleaning less of a chore. When you study the number of aftermarket parts available, it becomes obvious that the AR-15 rifle is the Mr. Potato Head of rifles. You may choose to make the rifle an ergonomically superior tool for short-range use, or to expend all effort on long-range perfection. A happy choice in the middle ground may be wise. Many shooters purchase a good quality rifle with the intention of upgrading it to personal taste. While many are good to go out-of-the-box from the standpoint of reliability, the sights, stock, and grip may leave something to be desired. Often a detail such as the stock is very important and makes

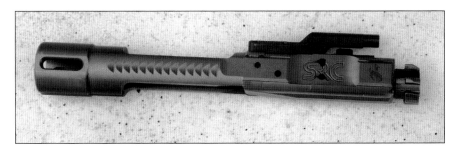

The Sharps Rifle Company bolt carrier is coated in space-age NP3. This is a good kit.

After being fired hundreds of rounds, a coated bolt carrier remains easily cleaned. NP3 is self-lubricating.

handling the rifle a better experience. It is important to purchase quality components. By choosing the best components—a good combination of parts is affordable with informed shopping—you will be able to improve the rifle's handling and be able to bond more closely with the rifle. Most of my parts come from Brownells.

AR-15 STOCKS

First, define your purpose and assess the mission. Do you have short or long arms? The stock should be durable. A high-impact polymer seems trouble free, but the better stocks offer the best rigidity. Mission First Tactical is never a bad choice. Rigidity is important. I like to be in control and do not want the stock to waver. A good stock from Brownells, my go-to source for AR-15 parts, is the B5 systems stock with storage components. If you run optics needing batteries, the B5 Systems is a good choice (100-009-033WB). I am particularly impressed with the Hogue buttstock. Ergonomic and rugged, the Hogue design is comfortable for extended firing. I like the locking device, as well. Decide if you like the type of release used for stock adjustment. The grip is personal. Some do not like the common finger stud; they feel it limits movement, but others want abrasion. The Hogue grip is popular and works

Hogue's round forend is a good first addition to a precision rifle.

The Hogue grip is offered in several good configurations.

Hogue Inc. offers a wide array of AR-15 accessories. Quality is good.

well in practice. Hogue offers a number of excellent designs. Magazines are another important consideration. I have used the Brownells Mil-Spec magazine with excellent results. Among polymer magazines the Magpul has earned an excellent reputation. You need to choose wisely, proof the magazines, and set back a quantity. Magazines are a renewable resource and should be replaced as necessary. Another replacement that is viable, but which demands much thought, is the trigger. Factory trigger actions are often heavy at six to eight pounds, and this limits control and accuracy. A crisp single-stage trigger compression is a great aid in accuracy, particularly in offhand fire.

I have used the Hiperfire Hipertouch trigger with excellent results. The Hiperfire trigger is delivered with two spring sets, the first for a trigger pull weight of 4 pounds-plus and the other for 6 pounds-plus. What drew me to this design is that the geometry of the trigger and hammer allow a light let-off, while the hammer fall is as heavy as Mil-Spec despite the lighter pull weight. In response to the problem of unburned powder, and other particles and debris potentially jamming the disconnect, the Hiperfire trigger has slots running the length of its bottom so that the disconnect will actually move debris from the trigger. The underside of the trigger has been raised and the end ramped up to increase the clearance between the trigger and the lower fire control cavity. According to Hiperfire, this will help prevent a blown primer cup or other debris from jamming the trigger. The trigger is installed with a minimum of work. Hiperfire recommends a 200-cycle dry-fire break-in. I performed this dry-fire break-in without any problem. To install the trigger, first clear the rifle and be certain that it isn't loaded. (If you do not already know this, you should not be handling firearms!) Next, break the action open and remove the upper assembly. Another tip—never allow the hammer to fall on the bolt catch. You could crack the frame. The lower receiver should be stabilized in a vise or block. Drive out the pins holding the trigger and hammer. Remove the trigger action. Assemble the Hiperfire trigger assembly. Now, place each side of the spring on the shoulder of the trigger. When the trigger goes into the receiver, the legs of the spring must be curved under the trigger and facing toward the front of the lower receiver. The disconnect spring will ride in the trigger in the circular cut-out. The larger end of the disconnect

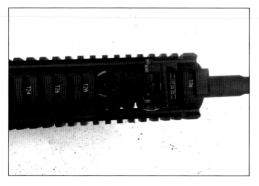

spring is down in the trigger, and the smaller tip is facing upward. A punch may be used to push this down properly. The disconnect rides the top of the disconnect spring so that the holes in the side line up with holes in the trigger. When you press the trigger pin in to secure the trigger action, be certain that it is flush with

Troy battle sights are arguably among the best of the breed.

each side of the receiver. Also, when ordering, be certain to order the correct parts. The Colt AR-15 takes a different trigger pin.

Ruger surprised the author by offering a high-quality drop-in trigger for their AR-556 series. While well suited to any AR-15 rifle, the Ruger uses small pins, 0.154 inch, so it will not fit the Colt. The Ruger Elite 452 MSR is a two-stage trigger. This trigger is delivered with a trigger press weight of 4.5 pounds, according to Ruger. My example breaks 4.6 pounds, so we are on the money, and it should smooth in with use. The 452 MSR uses a lightweight hammer to retain a full hammer strike. In order to ensure reliability, I like to use my own handloads using CCI Rifle Primers, which are traditionally hard primers. When using a rifle with a floating barrel, firing a hard primer is a

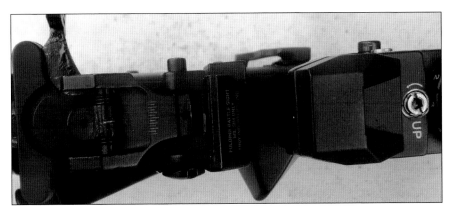

The Troy battle sights fold down neatly for storage or when optics are used.

good thing. Resistance to high pressure is also good. I added a number of steel cased loads in order to quality reliability. The Ruger 452 MSR is supplied with a safety selector and the springs and pins for installation. I was impressed that the trigger is delivered in a polymer approximation of the AR-15 firing handle. This makes for easy acclimation and dry-fire before installation. I am certain this assembly will be found in well-stocked shops, and that will more easily enable shooters to decide if they wish to install the lighter trigger in their personal rifles. The trigger was easily installed; no surprises there. While it would be suitable for any AR-15 with small pins, the Ruger AR 556 was the subject of this test. The trigger settled into 4.5 pounds after a bit of dry-fire. The rifle was test fired with a variety of handloads using the CCI rifle primer, and also with some steel cased loads. It was all *bang bang bang* and reliability established. Practical accuracy was improved, as well. This trigger action is new, but it passed the road test. As for precision fire, I was able to fire a group at 50 yards with the Federal 62-grain Green Tip, and another after fitting the trigger. Accuracy was improved on the order of perhaps a 25 percent smaller slow fire group, but the largest improvement was in offhand fire. The Ruger trigger action is worth its price.

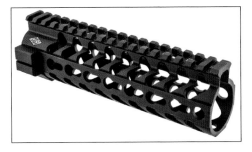

This Yankee Hill Machine forend from Brownells is useful and well made.

For precision fire at long range, and for a clean press, the Milazzo-Krieger MK II is a legendary trigger. It was introduced in the 1990s and went on to be used by the U.S. Army Marksmanship Unit. This was the only trigger used by the USAMU for some time. The trigger was out of production, but is now offered by Wisconsin Trigger Company. It demands a bit more finesse in installation. There is a set screw that is used to set the trigger, and the "wall" between the first and second stage is set by the user to his or her personal preference. This is a very well made and useful trigger unit.

SIGHTS

Some rifles are delivered without sights. Others have only rudimentary sights. I learned something about the durability of backup sights when mounting a set on my .308 rifle; they came apart. At present the Magpul seems durable and useful. The Wilson Combat steel sight is never a bad choice. When running a tactical firearm, it isn't right- or left-hand use that matters but forward or rear hand—the one in control at the moment. This means that an ambidextrous safety is important. At present the Badass (100-005-841WB—Brownells) seems ideal for tactical use. This is an inexpensive upgrade for rifles not delivered with an ambi safety. Handguards are another important consideration. If you are going to mount extensive gear you need a KeyMod type. One of the most popular from Brownells is

The Spikes Tactical build kit is great for builds, but also should be kept on hand just in case you need a spare part.

The BCM handguard is offered by Brownells. It works well and it is among the best of the modern forends.

the Yankee Hill Machine SKL. It is light at only 6.7 ounces, and made from 6061-T6 aluminum. Bravo Company also offers a popular handguard. Hogue offers a first-class round forend for those primarily interested in a free-floating target grade handguard. However, the design also offers some space for mounting combat lights or lasers. This is a good kit. GuntecUSA offers a classic round handguard I find useful. This is the ideal handguard for a dedicated long-range rifle.

OPTICS

You can spend more money on the optics than on the rifle, even given a quality rifle. I have used a number of rifle sights with good results. The Nikon M 223 features a reticule designed for long-range use. The reticule features sighting lines, represented by a wire below the middle reticule. These are small ballistic circles that represent the drop at certain, set yardage. It is a fast system to learn. Many of us like a Red Dot sight for combat use, and even for game shooting. The Burris AR-F3 is a strong favorite. In practical terms, the sight adds nothing to the weight of the gun at only .9 ounces. The sight is easily mounted and sighted in. Construction is simple and effective. There is a top cap for the battery. The elevation knob is at top, and both elevation and windage are adjustable with a coin. There is a power button for turning the sight on. Some practice is demanded in order to properly adjust the dot's brightness. The first setting is the automatic setting. A sensor at the front of the lens senses light from the target, and adjusts the red dot so that it is not overpowered by light from the target area. Next, press the power button again and you have the highest power setting. The next setting is a medium brightness, followed by the dimmest setting, and the next press of the button turns the sight's power off. You can change the setting quickly. I think that most of us will choose our ideal middle-of-the-road setting and leave it at that. I find the automatic setting works as designed, but I prefer to leave the Red Dot set for the medium setting. A colleague, a fine shot, leaves his Red Dot on maximum at all times. To each his own, and the AR-F3 clearly allows a good range of adjustment.

Redfield BattleZone

The BattleZone is a 3–9×42mm in standard format, with 6–18×44mm as an option. I chose the greater magnification of the 6–18×44mm for several reasons, including the proven accuracy of the Remington 700 and a bug for long-range shooting. Initial impressions were good. Focus is adjusted by means of a conventional twisting eye piece. The piece moved smoothly enough. I like a little effort involved as I do not wish the piece to twist without the intent for it to move. The interesting part of the scope is the Leupold CDS or Custom Dial System. (Leupold is Redfield's parent company.) These turrets allow fast adjustment for both range and windage. The BattleZone is supplied with two custom grade elevation dials. One is regulated for the performance of the .223 Remington using 55-grain projectiles at 3,100 fps. This is a common .223 loading. The second dial is regulated to the 168-grain 2,650 fps .308 Winchester load. I mounted the scope to the Remington Special Purpose Synthetic rifle, using DNZ one-piece mounts. These mounts have given excellent results in every application, and I use them on my bolt-action rifles. When you sight the rifle in with the standard load, you should be able to move the elevation and windage adjustments and get hits at 200–300 yards, with a 100-yard zero. However, if you are adept at counting clicks adjustment it is possible to connect at longer ranges, and due to the ergonomically designed turrets this may be done quickly. I find this quite useful with the .308. The flat shooting .223 requires less holdover, but as the range lengthens past several football fields even the .223 leaves the rifleman with a problem in accounting for drop. The scope does a good job of gathering light internally and offers excellent visibility. However, while the turrets are a great thing to have you actually have a combination of features that make getting long-range hits easier. For fast and dirty shooting at larger targets, the TAC MOA reticule features hash marks at 2-MOA spaced intervals. Along the vertical and horizontal crosswires, the visibility is very good. They may even be used for range estimation providing you know the height of the

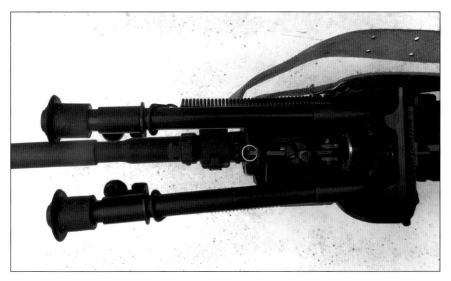

The Champion bipod has been proven reliable, durable, and stable.

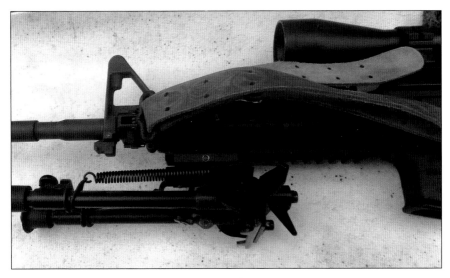

The Champion bipod rides on the author's SOCOM Colt.

target you are engaging. I also have the Redfield BattleZone on my personal Colt SOCOM. This is a good kit.

BOLT CARRIER

Sharps Rifle Company introduced the bolt carrier to eliminate any issue with the AR-15 bolt carrier assembly. The rotational camming of the carrier during the unlocking portion of the operational cycle was addressed, along with canting of the bolt carrier group upon firing due to the gas pressure exerted to the gas key, which naturally causes the front of the bolt carrier group to rise and the rear of the bolt carrier group to be pressed downward during its rearward travel. SRC used computer design technology, coupled with real world testing, to address both of these issues. The Sharps BBC is machined from S7 heat-treated steel. The carrier is finished inside and out with NP3/NP3 PLUS to minimize the need for lubricants, to aid in smooth operation, and to make clean-up easy. This process co-deposits sub-micron particles of PTFE (polytetrafluoroethylene), commonly known as Teflon, for self-lubricating corrosion resistance. NP3 PLUS offers corrosion resistance for marine and other hostile environments. I have used this carrier in a number of rifles, but presently it rides in my go-to Colt SOCOM. This is a good kit and well worth the money.

MAGAZINES

There are many operational decisions to be made. Rifle and ammunition selection should be based on concrete observational data. Magazines are a renewable resource and should be discarded when they become nonfunctional. Magazine maintenance involves inspecting magazines and occasionally removing lint and debris. For the most part, magazines should be trashed rather than repaired, at least at the current price of magazines. If they reach the panic levels of a few years ago, then we may indeed become repair experts. The

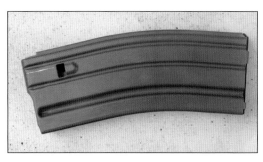

This is the Brownells magazine. This is as good at it gets.

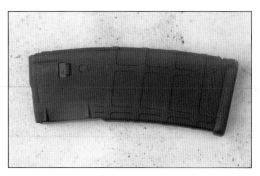

The Polymer PMAG has given excellent service.

best program is to stock up on as many quality magazines as soon as possible. I am going to tell you how to spot a quality magazine, and how to separate the service grade from the junk grade. I will also point out the magazines that have provided good service.

The AR-15 magazine should use a modern anti-tilt follower. This follower simply keeps the magazines properly aligned and prevents snagging the nose of the magazine during the feed cycle. Next, examine the magazine. Magazines are sheet metal aluminum stampings. They are joined together; in the areas where the folds join, the magazine should be smooth without protrusions. Burrs or uneven areas inside the magazine will catch the follower or the cartridge, and the result will be to stop proper feeding. Again: The two overlapping pieces should be smooth; a sloppy metal fold results in a failure to feed. Polymer magazines are made differently, but here again, polymer extrusions on the inside of the magazine will stop feeding. There are differences in the overall length of the cartridge that affect feeding, and a problematic magazine adds to the problem. A JSP or FMJ bullet will usually feed well in all rifles and with all but the worst magazines. The open tip bullets will snag on an off spec or poorly made magazine. Be certain to proof every magazine in use. GI magazines with the new-style green follower are the best of the GI types. The cartridges are kept level, and this prevents a double feed. The magazine should have no play in the follower, and the magazine should drop free of the magazine well when the magazine release is actuated.

Feed lips are usually made well enough for good function unless the magazine has been dropped and damaged. Brownells offers a magazine lip gauge similar to a Go/No-Go headspace gauge in operation, and it will save a lot of time in isolating junk or damaged magazines. Be certain the magazine has sufficient clearing for the bullet nose inside the magazine body. There are also occasional energy problems encountered with certain loads that will show up on magazines. The 36- to 40-grain varmint loads in .223 do not always function properly in the AR-15. There isn't enough momentum. A weak magazine spring will exhibit greater problems with these loads. Do not overload the magazine. It is possible to get twenty-one cartridges in some twenty-round magazines and thirty-one in some thirty-round magazines. But there is no point in overloading. It might be that the magazine would not seat when inserted in the magazine well under a closed bolt when overloaded. In fact, the opposite may be true. For many years, it has been common wisdom to load the AR-15 magazine *down* for best reliability. This means eighteen rounds in the twenty-round magazines and twenty-eight rounds in the thirty-round magazines. There are many shooters who have fired thousands of rounds from magazines, and who feel this is a necessary practice. Some of these are combat veterans. According to an engineer friend, relieving the magazine by two rounds relieves pressure by more than 10 percent—more like 20 percent—although removing any more than that reaches a point of diminishing returns. If you are going on deployment with the newest magazines, then the Sergeant is right; they are completely reliable fully loaded. For the rest of us engaged in mundane pursuits, loading a few rounds down doesn't hurt. As for high capacity magazines of forty rounds and more, I have yet to see one that met my reliability standards. Because of weight and handling issues, I am not willing to pay a high price for an unreliable instrument. Among the most proven magazines are the quality aluminum

The Specter sling has given the author good results on several rifles.

magazines from Brownells. The Brownells brand won a grueling military competition. These are affordable and have given excellent service. Some prefer polymer magazines. I have enjoyed excellent service with both the PMAG and Troy magazines. In aluminum magazines, the Colt, NHMGT, OKAY, and Brownells magazines are excellent examples of quality magazines. In polymer, the PMAG is a great choice.

SLINGS

The Blue Force Vickers Tactical sling gave good service during the months I worked with AR-15 rifles. I am certain some find single-point slings useful; however, they are not the marksmanship aid that a good standard sling can be. Nor do they allow the user muzzle control with the sling. The Specter slings have given excellent results as far as retention is concerned, and also with regard to marksmanship.

A few notes: A number of things made this book go more smoothly. The GPS magazine pouch from Brownells holds eight magazines. This is invaluable when heading to the range. Also from Brownells was the ATI Universal Bipod that I used. When comparing different rifles, this bipod offered a quick-change option that kept me shooting and shooting accurately.

Green or red laser? The choice is yours.

CHAPTER SEVENTEEN

OPTICS FOR THE DEFENSIVE RIFLE

Rifle optics are an important consideration. You can spend as much or more on the rifle scope as on the rifle itself. Money invested in quality optics is well spent. When you begin searching for an optic it is good to consult experienced shooters. See what they have used in the hunting field or in three-gun competitions. Chances are you will hear positive comments about many good brands and negative comments on a few others. One negative on a name like Nikon or Redfield isn't a deal changer, but a consistent bad report card on an inexpensive optic would have me looking somewhere else. In this section, I am going to cover a few of the rifle scopes that have served me well, but for the most part I am going to outline the options so that you will be able to make good choices for *your* personal situation.

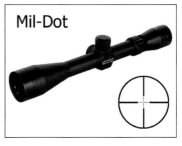

The Mil-Dot reticule offered by Leopold is perhaps the most popular tactical reticule.

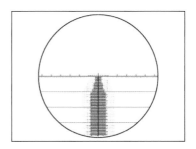

Before choosing a reticule, be certain it will prove versatile and suitable for your type of shooting.

The offerings include quite a range of type, price, and performance. The choice can be difficult and the catalogs can take up a lot of time if read thoroughly. I cannot decide on a scope for you, but I can outline the choices available in a rifle scope, and then you may choose one that fits your specific needs. A good idea would be for you to write down a list of criteria before you begin shopping for a scope. Be completely honest about your anticipated needs.

QUESTIONS YOU SHOULD CONSIDER

- Will the scope be used primarily for home defense or area defense? Are you a peace officer with a requirement the scope must co-witness? Will you be using the scope in three-gun competition?
- What is the range you anticipate using the scope for in the majority of shooting, and what is the expected maximum range? Examples: A rifle fitted with a Red Dot that is a great scope to 50 yards or so. It suits my needs as a truck gun. I don't want to be helpless with this rifle at 100 yards.
- Will any of the shooting be dim light shooting, as in predator calling?
- What type and caliber is the rifle? Is recoil a significant factor?
- How heavy is the rifle? How much weight will the rifle scope add?
- What is your budget?

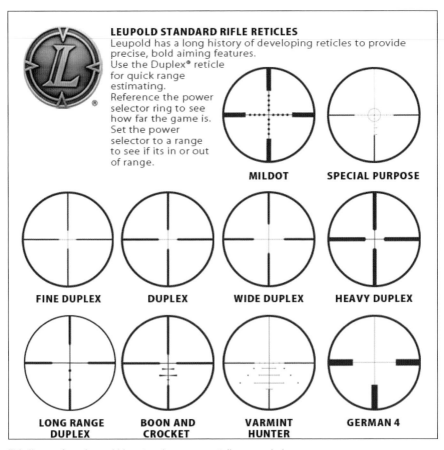

This line-up from Leupold is extensive; you can tailor your choice.

SPECIALIZED SCOPES

Some rifle scopes are more versatile than others, and some are specialized. You may need a specialized scope for varmint hunting or predator calling, or as a close quarter red dot. I think that possibly the most useful of all rifle scopes is a good quality variable magnification type. The fixed magnification scope is often rugged and simple, but it lacks versatility. The variable power scope allows adjusting the field of view and exit pupil. On that subject, how much magnification is needed? You do not need much magnification to shoot accurately at common rifle ranges of 50 to 250 yards. Four power is good. I have used a Nikon 20X, and while the brilliantly clear optic was a joy to use at 500 yards, it was something I seldom did. The lowest setting was the most common as I fired the rifle at 1 to 200 yards. A small field of view is inherent with a high-power scope. You may have a difficult time finding a small target, or even a deer's vitals. Getting on and engaging a white target, such as the Innovative Targets steel reaction target, is simple with the 4X scope at 200 yards, while finding a buff-colored deer at the same range might be more difficult. I like to think of the higher magnification as a good setting for identification, while 4X is just about ideal for most shooting. The 3–9X power hunting scope is perfect for most uses. Let's consider field of view. This is defined as the area you will perceive when looking through the rifle scope at a certain power setting. The higher the magnification the less field of view. Manufacturer specifications are a big help in this regard; and they will give you detailed information about field of view and magnification. If you need a spotting scope, then get a good one. A rifle scope and a spotting scope do different things; the spotting scope is more powerful. I do not like glassing the hills for game with a rifle that may be pointed at another hunter. Take into consideration that magnification and objective lens size are related. If you are firing only in good light at the firing range or in competition, then light gathering attributes are not important However, if you are hunting under normal conditions—in the brush, under trees, sometimes with an overcast sky—light gathering can be very important. The brighter the better, say some of my experienced friends. If the scope features an objective lens of 40mm with a 10X magnification power, you have a 4mm exit pupil. You divide the objective diameter by the magnification to determine exit pupil. If the lens is set at a lower setting—say 4X—then you have a

When firing for accuracy, the author found the Vanguard rifle scope to be excellent and well worth its price.

10mm exit pupil. Magnification makes for a lower field of view. A 50mm objective lens may have greater clarity, but for most shooters the 40mm lens is ideal.

Turret adjustment is an important consideration. These turrets are necessary for effective windage and elevation adjustments. Some feature audible clicks; I fear I no longer hear them for painfully obvious reasons. Scopes are provided with ¼ and ½ to 1 minute of angle adjustment. I think that the 1 MOA setting is fine enough for most of us, and like the quarter MOA better. The turrets must feature a solid cap and good stop adjustment. At present I am using two examples of the Vanguard 4–12×40mm, and this scope is ideal for my personal use. It should be suitable for yours, as well. Once you have nailed down the scope you wish to use, and have decided upon the magnification and other features, you may wish to consider the reticule. The standard cross hairs reticule works well for most of us. The only type I have used that I found counterproductive was a type that features a post with a dot on top. My eyes did not center the post properly and, frankly, I consider it only a step up from iron sights. A reticule is simply a crosshair, or point of aim, inside the scope. The first step in using the scope properly is to adjust the eyepiece so that you are able to see the reticule clearly. (Only very few eyepieces are not adjustable.) Turn the ring until the reticule appears sharp in your vision.

Vanguard offers an extensive line of scopes that work well for hunting.

When looking through a scope at one of the larger stores you will see quite a few reticule designs. Cabela's, for example, will have a dozen or so different types of popular scopes on display. By adjusting the locking ring on a display model, you may move the scope with your hand until you have found the proper focus. Then you will consider which reticule suits your needs and shooting style. There are different sizes of crosshairs from fine to heavy. Duplex and tactical reticules have different designs. The heavier type shows up against the target in low light. Against the background of a game animal a heavy outline is best. The smallest lines are suited to long-range fire. The finer crosshair will cover only a small part of the target. A scope intended for hunting deer at 100 yards has a different role in the scheme of things than a scope intended for use at several hundred yards to explode varmints. When using iron sights, the front post may obscure the target completely because the rifle scope subtends so much area with its crosshairs. The amount of the target the crosshair covers is the subtension, a good term to understand. When you adjust the power or magnification of the lens, the crosshair doesn't enlarge because the crosshairs are located in the second plane. (This is true with very few exceptions.) Subtension decreases as the rifle scope

When you are many miles from a warranty station, a good rifle scope is worth its weight in gold.

magnification is cranked up. As for the exact size of the reticule, there are many proprietary types. I like well-defined reticules. Those with hashmarks for connecting at different ranges are useful, but not completely necessary.

I like the design, however, and both my Remington 700 tactical rifle and the Colt AR-15 rifle wear Redfield BattleZone scopes with this feature. A lot of your range work should be devoted to discovering exactly where the point of impact will be when using these marks. Just because the zero is 100 yards,

Proper eye relief and focus are an important part of rifle scope selection.

and the first mark above the center is supposed to have your bullet dead-on at 125 yards, it may not work in the field with your load. Most are surprisingly accurate, and there is a lot of R&D behind the designs, but test this at the range. Be certain that you have confirmed the point of aim and point of impact. In most cases the hash mark is dead-on when using standard loads. Remember, some ranging marks are helpful, but not at the expense of a crowded and busy field of view.

Red Dot Sights

Red dot sights are zero power or no magnification. They are not for long precision shooting, but instead are for close-range, very fast shooting. As an example, with most red dots the dot itself will subtend about 4 inches at 100 yards. However, some are accurate enough for 100 yards shooting. Simply put the red dot on the target and you get a hit. The dot is imaged in a holographic display on a screen. These sights are fast for close-range battle. In some cases, they are useful for predators and pests, as well. Let's look at some of the better examples. Red dot sights are plentiful and the choices may be confusing. Some are cheap products best suited to .22 caliber rimfire firearms. Others are service grade and often expensive. While quality is never a bad investment, most of us are interested in a

A red dot demands different discipline. This humble Tasco is a good training aid.

This old Tasco has been on quite a few AR rifles.

durable sight with good features at an affordable price. Inexpensive red dots are useful as trainers, but the better types are the right choice for personal defense and hunting. All of us have budgets, some larger than others, and many of us have been burned by a cheap product. Buy cheap, buy twice is a truism. The Burris FastFire 3 is an affordable, useful red dot sight from a respected name. No single optic is a "go anywhere, do anything" choice for every rifle, but the AR-F3 is useful and versatile. I find the red dot especially well-suited to personal defense; others will find it a good beginning at three-gun matches. This sight is a good choice for predators and varmints at

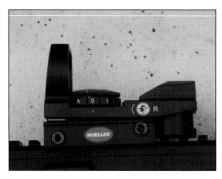

The Mueller Red Dot gave good performance in its price range.

moderate range in the Ranch Rifle niche. The AR-F3 features magnification of 1.07X, which offers an excellent field of view. With magnification, the use of both eyes at once—an important advantage in personal defense shooting—is nullified. A lack of magnification is an advantage in this type of shooting. The strength of the sight is that the tunnel vision which occurs with a tube-type sight using both eyes is eliminated. *The intent with a red dot sight is to allow an open field of view while the red dot is superimposed on the target.* The red dot covers 4 MOA at 100 yards. The AR-F3 mounts easily on a standard Picatinny rail. The sight window is 21×15mm. Adjustment range allows good sighting in to 100 yards, or slightly more. Both elevation and adjustment are generous with the range of degree 190 inches at 100 yards.

When setting the zero, remember that the dials move the red dot. When setting elevation for "up," the red dot actually moves upwards. Also, a rather coarse zero at moderate range of 25 yards or so may not be accurate at 100 yards, so be certain to confirm zero and keep the rifle sighted for the most likely engagement range. With the red dot sighted on my personal Smith & Wesson Military and Police Sport rifle, I decided to give the sight a good workout. I began with a good supply of High Precision Downrange (HPR) 55-grain FMJ loads. I also used several JSP loads from the same maker. I would not hesitate to use the loads from this company for any type of critical use. I spent some time at the bench in zeroing the rifle for 200 yards, and

The Burris Red Dot gets the nod for the author's personal rifle.

doing so at 25 yards using proven technique. With an AR-15 rifle, with 16-inch barrel zeroed for a 200-yard target, the rifle remains versatile for all around use. On the other hand, the rifle zeroed for 15 yards is ridiculously high at 50–100 yards and far less useful. Fourteen inches high at 100 yards is difficult to account for! As an example, if the rifle is sighted for 200 yards then the bullet will strike about 3 inches low at 10 yards.

If you have to pull off a hostage rescue shot, then aim for the brow of the head, not the center of the eyes. At 50 yards, you are about 0.3 inch low, about 1.1 inches high at 100 yards, and then dead-on again at 200 yards with the high velocity .223 cartridge. This is the rule with standard 55-grain FMJ and 55-grain JSP loads. In the end, the 200-yard zero is ideal for most uses, but you must confirm your zero at the range. The Burris AR-F3 is most useful in fast-moving shooting at ranges of 10–50 yards. This is definitely the long end of any likely engagement. I found the sight gets on target quickly. Over the course of several weeks, the rifle was carried behind the seat of the truck and handled with respect but not babied, and fired well over four hundred rounds, primarily HPR 55-grain FMJ. The combination is a credible

For those just getting their feet wet in red dots, the Aim Sports red dot worked fine.

one. The Burris red dot sight seems capable of holding the zero, hitting the target when combined with practice, and offers good economy for the performance.

I have enjoyed good results with the Mueller Optics tactical scopes, and wished to try the Quick Shot Waterproof Red Dot. This is a design I mounted on my most advanced AR-15. With a Spikes Tactical receiver this rifle uses Troy back-up sights that co-witness with the Red Dot. The Mueller uses dual sensors

The ATN X-Sight is among the most advanced optics on the planet and well suited for the enthusiast.

to detect surrounding light conditions and automatically adjusts the brightness of the dot to these conditions. This seems to be the trend among new red dots, to use automatic light compensation. There are also four different reticle styles available, which is unusual. This is the newest optic on any of my rifles, and the Spikes Tactical on my newest AR-15 rifle. I like the combination a lot. This is one of those happy combinations that invites shooters to take it to the range and practice until they excel.

TruGlo Tactical Illuminated Riflescope

TruGlo designed this scope to offer a combination of clarity, precision, and speed. The scope is designed to offer a bridge between the speed of a red dot and the precision of a rifle scope. As such there are inherent compromises, but for use at 25–125 yards the scope works well. The tube is 30mm rather than 1 inch. This makes for increased

This Remington .223 is fitted with a Redfield scope. It will do the job well past 150 yards. The primary limitation is the shooter.

brightness and a larger range of adjustment. They are offered in 1–4×24mm and 1–6×24mm. Either will do a good job, and while 99 percent of my shooting will be covered by the 1–4X scope, consider your needs and the 1–6X may be your best bet. The lenses are multi-coated. I have tested this scope extensively on one of my favorite rifles. The mix of clarity and contrast is good. I find this scope to be one of the fastest to a rapid hit that I have used. The scope has a wide field of

The Redfield BattleZone scope is well suited to the author's personal use and rides on several rifles.

view, which for some invites shooting with both eyes open. If you are young and can adapt, this is the way to go with red dot scopes—and this goes as well when set at 1X. Sometimes you need 4X, and the 6X scope allows rapid zooming by virtue of an innovative lever incorporated into the design. The

A Battle Company Rifle, Redfield Optics, and Fiocchi ammunition—a good kit and very accurate.

scope is supplied with a monolithic one-piece scope mount. While the scope is intended for the AR-15 market, there is no reason it would not be a great companion to any rifle with proper mounts. This scope also has pre-calibrated adjustment turrets for ranges up to 400 yards. The TruGlo scope is a lot of scope for the money. It may not be the scope for critical use, but then again I have experienced no problems in several months of use. For most of what we do with a rifle and a scope, the TruGlo is a good kit.

During the course of my shooting career I have used many optics. Some were store brands, some were no-names with chain store logos. I tend to keep an inexpensive rifle scope handy for use with new rifles. I also have scopes that have been more reliable than the rifles, but still, the inexpensive rifle scope is good to have.

The Nikko Stirling line has given good service and is backed with a fine warranty. I had no complaint in using the Nikko Stirling to test several rifles. However, during the work on this book I experienced a detached reticle with

The author has tested a number of inexpensive optics. While the Nikko Stirling worked okay, the reticule separated during an extensive firing session.

The author cannot compliment a scope higher than the Meopta hunting, tactical, range scope.

Meopta scopes offer excellent value and consistent performance.

a Nikko Stirling. Then again, after firing forty-five rounds of .308 as quickly as possible, I suppose this wasn't unexpected. Something more rugged is needed for hard use.

I elected to replace the scope originally fitted to the Ruger/Straight-Jacket rifle with a Meopta 3–9×40mm. The scope is available in many versions, the most versatile of which may be the HTR, or Hunt, Tactical, Range. This scope offers European quality at a fair price. I have enjoyed excellent results. So it seems I mounted a cheap scope, found it unacceptable, and then mounted an excellent scope. Not an uncommon thing to do, but not the most cost efficient. The Meopta line is well worth your consideration. This is perhaps the finest and, overall, most useful scope I have used in testing rifles in the months preceding the publication of this work.

I have used an inexpensive Redfield Revolution for some time with excellent results. While two hundred dollars isn't pocket change, it isn't a thousand-dollar scope. It has ridden on several rifles, notably the Remington 799 in .223. This is a scope with clear optics and excellent adjustments, well worth its price. I would buy another and certainly recommend it. Other scopes have better resolution, but for the price the Redfield is a good scope.

I have also used the Redfield BattleZone on several rifles. I had information that the BattleZone was being discontinued for an improved model, but just before I finished this chapter I checked and many are available at several outlets. The BattleZone is a great

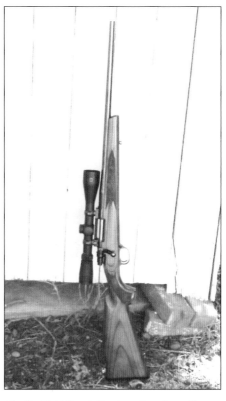

The Redfield Revolution has given the author good service on several bolt-action rifles.

scope for the money—about three hundred dollars—and I enjoy using it.

Nikon offers the M223 with many good features that we have come to expect from this maker. Nitrogen filled, waterproof, fog and shockproof, and O-ring sealed. Many scopes have some version of a drop compensator. The

Time and again, the Redfield BattleZone has given good results.

The Nikon M-223 is among the consistently excellent rifle scopes tested.

Rapid Action Turret is Nikon's drop compensating feature. This system is based on the 55-grain .223, but has proven useful with other loads. Simply turn the turret and you can compensate for drop up to 600 yards. While crosshair holdover works, the RATT certainly makes life easier.

CHAPTER EIGHTEEN

MAINTENANCE

FIXING COMMON PROBLEMS

When it comes to maintenance the basics include proper cleaning and lubrication. However, most of our concerns will focus on the AR-15 rifle. The AR-15 is fired the most, used hard, and modified often. The AR-15 is America's

rifle, and the black rifle is a great firearm with a hard-earned reputation for reliability. Problems with the AR-15 system are usually traced to poor maintenance and ammunition selection. The US Army made mistakes with the rifle, using a powder combination that results in unreliable operation. Without writing another book to cover this debacle, I will simply state that Congress called the events "Criminal Negligence." The AR-15 got a black eye for unreliability and it took some time to recover. The Army finally corrected the problem. When service rifles were used with corrosive primed ammunition, maintenance demands were more severe than they are today. The M1 .30 carbine was the first low maintenance rifle, but this was possible only because the carbine was used with non-corrosive ammunition. When the term low maintenance is used, it does not mean the shooter is free from cleaning and lubrication chores; it means that the chores are not as difficult as with other rifles. The logical progression from black powder to smokeless powder to

A basic field strip is okay for general maintenance and cleaning, but a more detailed disassembly is required at periodic intervals.

Don't think it is clean—be certain it is clean!

non-corrosive primers has led to modern rifles that are very reliable, and which demand little maintenance. The modern situation isn't without historical precedent. The first assault rifle in many ways was the Henry 1860 rifle. A tremendous advancement at the time, the Henry fell victim to black powder residue and an exposed feed system that was easily jammed, and which frequently clogged. Perfect maintenance isn't always possible in the field.

The AR-15 chamber gets dirty, so be certain you have it good and clean.

Corrosive salts that were present in priming compounds prior to World War II meant a much more stringent cleaning regiment for the M1 Garand and all of the machine guns in use. Within the limitations of its caliber and range the M1 carbine was a great step forward, but ammunition technology made the AR-15 possible. So, we have a modern rifle that is user friendly, accurate, and reliable. But the rifle must be cleaned. We tend to fire these rifles a lot, and that means a lot of powder ash. Copper fouling builds up. The cheapest ammunition is often the dirtiest, so decide right from the beginning if you are willing to go the extra mile in using ammunition from countries that may not have our powder technology. On the other

This is an AR-15 chamber sopping wet with powder solvent.

hand, all brands will leave heavy deposits with enough firing, so cleaning must be done. Clean the rifle as if your life hung in the balance, because it just may be true at some point. I have a regimen that I follow in cleaning a rifle. Due to the design of the AR-15, it is more than simply cleaning the barrel, chamber, and bolt. The trigger group must be cleaned along with the barrel and chamber. The entire operating mechanism must be cleaned, and this includes the trigger group, bolt carrier, chamber, and bore. I begin with an aerosol spray, but this doesn't do the entire job. The bolt and carrier are removed and then thoroughly cleaned. I use professional grade cleaning kits with scrub brushes for attacking the grime on the bolt carrier and the action.

Be certain that each of the teeth of the AR-15 bolt is clean and free of carbon.

A tie-up will take the fun out of a rifle match or an expensive hunt, and you may end up at the morgue with a toe tag in a gunfight. Even if you do not use the rifle for critical use, pride of ownership demands that the rifle be clean and lubricated and ready for action. The rifle may function with a minimal amount of carbon buildup, but then again it may not, depending upon how tight the rifle is. After all, we like our rifles tighter than the military standard. The locking lugs demand attention and carbon buildup must be removed. There are tools that can be used which include purpose-designed picks to nudge out carbon from hard-to-get-to areas. Normal wear in a rifle means that it will fire tens of thousands of cartridges without any problem. Damage called "eccentric wear" caused by a lack of cleaning is another matter, and once it starts eccentric wear worsens quickly. It isn't dissimilar to a scarred piston in a Chevy.

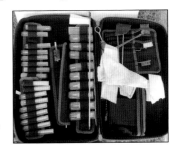

This is a rather neat cleaning kit that covers rifles, pistols, and shotguns—and it wasn't expensive. Brownells or Cheaper than Dirt are top choices for such kits.

When a malfunction is experienced on the firing range, you need to address the issue. I would first look to the magazine, and test the rifle with another magazine. If problems continue, do the best job possible in cleaning the rifle. Next, examine the extractor and extractor spring. The extractor spring may need to be replaced. Another problem may be the ammunition. It isn't exactly a malfunction, but often enough a shooter will complain of poor accuracy. The rifle isn't at its best. This is a particular concern when the rifle has previously been accurate, but then loses its edge. The first concern when you want to restore accuracy is to be certain the rifle has a clean bore. When the rifle demonstrates poor accuracy, the problem is seldom a shot-out barrel. I have not seen a shot-out AR-15 barrel, although I have seen many that have been fouled so badly that accuracy suffers. The steps to alleviate this problem are simple. The bore must be thoroughly cleaned using a good bore solvent and the wet and dry patch method. A lot of effort will be required to clean the rifle, but in the end, it should be able to be restored to good accuracy potential. If this cleaning doesn't bring the rifle up to standard, then you may have a deeper problem, such as a damaged barrel crown.

A well-packed box defies organization at times! Cleaning patches and solvent are essential.

Having a muzzle brake doesn't mean the muzzle crown cannot be damaged; improper cleaning tools may still damage the muzzle. But if that does happen, the barrel can be re-crowned. If this is the difficulty, some of us like to test the rifle with a magazine full of different loads. This works fine as long as you remember the respective staggering of the ammunition. A type of ammunition I avoid for most uses is steel-cased loads. Many have a polymer coating that gets hot, becomes soft, and may adhere to the rifle's chamber. When the coating has melted steel-cased loads remain

Sharp Shoot R offers an excellent cleaning kit. Just use it properly!

reliable, but once you switch to brass cartridge cases the sticky chamber seems to catch the brass. It's true that steel-cased loads are an inexpensive resource, but be aware of such drawbacks.

LUBRICATION

Keep the rifle properly lubricated. There are a number of stages involved in proper lubrication. The first is *storage,* when the rifle is lightly oiled, in order to discourage corrosion. The rifle should normally be stored muzzle down. The next stage is *combat ready*, when the bolt carrier should be lubricated. The next stage is *range work*. In this type of shooting the rifle is kept sopping wet with lubrication. In a defensive or hunting situation only a few cartridges will be fired, but in a competition or range setting you may fire hundreds in the course of a single day. It is important to keep the rifle lubricated during these firing drills. A rifle that is at the ready for taking out pests and varmints, or the dedicated home defense rifle, may only be lightly lubricated; the rifle going to a competition or lengthy training

If you use quality ammunition, the rifle will burn cleaner and you will have far fewer malfunctions.

session should be more heavily lubricated. If you have fired a hundred cartridges or so during practice, it is a good idea to throw more lubricant on the bolt carrier before you continue. Another concern that is sometimes addressed with the AR-15 rifle is the trigger action becoming inconsistent. This is a common problem, and the most popular cause is some type of debris in the action. The trigger will be inconsistent which simply means that the trigger

These steel-cased loads were subjected to moisture during a magazine test. Judge for yourself.

break will register different pull weights for each press of the trigger. A good cleaning will most often cure this problem of grit in the mechanism. (The Hiperfire trigger is designed to avoid this pitfall.) Almost always, when dealing with the AR-15 rifle the real problem is a lack of cleaning or lubrication. Another sore spot is AR-15 magazines. Some are of good quality but are just worn out. Magazines are a renewable resource and you cannot simply change the magazine spring and straighten the body in every situation. Sometimes it is time to trash the magazines. Some of the polymer magazines warp, crack, and get out of spec. But so do the aluminum magazines. If the magazine is dropped and feed lips are bent, then the magazine must be discarded. Your life is worth more than the modest cost of a new PMAG. A final concern is the AR-15 gas ring.

These gas rings must be in serviceable order to work properly. The standard test is to remove the carrier group from the rifle and place the bolt carrier group on the work bench. The carrier should support its own weight. If it collapses on itself, the gas rings need changing. With the gas rings in good shape, proper lubrication, and quality magazines, the AR-15 rifle is a model of reliability. The next step is to use ammunition in the proper specification. I cover the choices in ammunition in another chapter.

THE UPPER—KEEPING THINGS ROLLING

The AR-15 rifle is a modular design that can be quickly changed to other calibers by adding a complete upper unit. While individual parts are easily changed, the entire caliber can also be changed. The easiest way to do this is by obtaining a complete upper assembly. I have looked over some of the better units and found examples in 6.5 Grendel, 6.8 SPC, 7.62×39mm and .300 BAC. Which one makes the most sense isn't the real question, but rather which one *you* personally like and feel will be an enjoyable unit to fire and use becomes the right choice. As far as ammunition costs are concerned, the 7.62×39mm is a viable option, but for specialized use the .300 Blackout (BAC) is a good bet. For myself, the .300 Blackout has

The wrong place to go cheap is on the magazine! This one works fine.

My local UPS store printed these labels for marking magazines. Keeping up with malfunctions isn't possible otherwise.

some interest and I have used this conversion most often. The ability to use the standard issue AR-15 bolt and magazine is appealing. Just be careful; do not load the .300 cartridge case into a .223 rifle!

SPECIFIC MAINTENANCE TIPS
Ruger 10/22 Maintenance

One of the first rifles in the battery, and one we must have, is the Ruger 10/22 .22 caliber self-loading rifle. The Ruger enjoys a fine reputation for low-maintenance reliability and accuracy. The Rugers I have encountered that have not been reliable are ones which have been abused or fitted with poor quality aftermarket parts. All rifles age and require maintenance, but the Ruger 10/22 is one that is low on the list for problems. When a Ruger 10/22 gives trouble the first thing to check is the ammunition. Are you using bargain basement grade loads that are really no bargain? The Winchester Super X will burn clean and give good function. Using quality high-velocity ammunition with a bullet weight of 37 to 40 grains works. Accuracy is pretty much standard in these rifles. An off-the-shelf Ruger 10/22 in the standard wood stock configuration with a factory trigger action will usually group three shots of Winchester 40-grain .22 LR into 2–3 inches at 50 yards. For

small game hunting, pests, and informal target practice this is a good standard. The long suit of this rifle is relia-bility. The blowback action is simple and doesn't give trou-ble. But the most interesting part of the Ruger is the ten-round rotary magazine. Bill Ruger was impressed by the Savage 99 magazine and

This cartridge did a 360 and tried to enter the chamber backwards! Whether a weak spring or poor ammo, the problem should be studied each time a malfunction occurs.

modeled his 10/22 magazine after this standard. This feed device has proved reliable and seems never to give trouble. If the Ruger magazine malfunctions, discard it and obtain another. There have been a host of high-capacity after-market magazines introduced. I have tested many of these plastic magazines and have never found an example that is reliable. Some work okay for a few hundred cartridges; some do not. The Ruger factory magazine is a model of excellent function. Ruger finally offered a twenty-five-round factory product. I have less experience with this magazine than the many ten-round maga-zines I have tested, but I find it to be reliable and nothing I have heard dimin-ishes this opinion. If you desire more than ten rounds, then the Ruger maga-zine is a must have.

The simplest means of improving 10/22 accuracy is to install a heavy match barrel. This is easily done. The Green Mountain barrels I have used are heavier and more accurate than the factory product. They are well worth their price. The stock is important. The Hogue OverMolded is a great fit and gives excellent utility. Many cheap plastic stocks are less than ideal. Some of the stock kits that are offered for the Ruger 10/22 look racy, some look space age and can be fun to use, but they are not usually a good fit. Some even cause the rifle to rattle after the stock is fitted. There is no bedding to speak of and stability is poor. The rifle's accuracy is often lost with such a contraption. If plinking at 25 yards is the goal then it is okay, but otherwise these stocks are poor choices. (An exception is the ScottWerx conversion.) The Hogue stock is a better choice. As for the Ruger rifle, I think that it may be said that a certain amount of accuracy is sacrificed for long-term reliability. Just the same, the Ruger is accurate enough for most chores and is probably the least demanding rifle in this book from the standpoint of maintenance .

There are a few tips that will keep a rifle running. When you insert a rotary magazine, make certain it is properly seated. A firm insertion is needed, and be certain that the magazine snaps into place. This is necessary for proper feed reliability. When removing the magazine, actuate the magazine release and let the magazine fall into your hand. Operating the bolt lock is sometimes confusing, but it needn't be. When loading the rifle, be certain to pull the bolt to the rear and let it snap forward. Working the bolt slowly may not smoothly load the rifle. The bolt lock lever is pressed in to lock the bolt to the rear, and it is pressed to allow the bolt to run forward.

M1A1 Rifles

If any rifle covered in this pages deserves to be called a rifleman's rifle it is the Springfield M1A1. This is a great rifle with much to recommend. The Springfield M1A1 has done excellent work in competition, and in the original M14 form it continues to serve as a battle rifle. The M1A1 is a descendant of the M1 Garand. For proper function, this rifle demands cleaning and lubrication, and only with proper attention to detail will this rifle continue to be reliable. To field strip the rifle, first drop the magazine, and then rack the bolt and triple check the chamber. Lock the bolt to the rear and set the magazine aside. Next, hold the rifle and control the action as the rifle is turned with the magazine well facing the shooter. The trigger guard itself is pressed upward to release the barrel action. At times the trigger guard is stiff and difficult to unlatch, especially with a newer rifle, but with enough effort the sheet metal trigger guard will pop open. A padded bar for leverage may help with a good tight rifle that is just out of the box. With the trigger guard open, the barreled action is simply pulled out of the stock. For cleaning and maintenance, this is all that is usually needed. The only problem I have seen in high-round count rifles is the incidence of corrosion around the gas port. This may be due to seasonal exposure, or perhaps corrosive salts in the priming compound of corrosive primed ammunition. It isn't an attractive proposition to add a requirement to clean the rifle, even when a few rounds are fired, and to me this outweighs the low cost of surplus ammunition. By the same token, cartridges with a steel cartridge case put more pressure on the extractor. In my experience, Springfield M1A1 rifles come out of the box shooting and with good accuracy. The occasional stock doesn't fit properly, but bedding the stock properly will cure this uncommon problem. A big problem is off-specification magazines. I have ordered the proper Springfield magazine from Brownells to ensure function. I have never seen an off-brand magazine that worked properly in a Springfield M1A1 without modification.

AK-47 Maintenance

The AK-47 rifle is a model of reliability, ruggedness, and hardy combat ability. But this rifle also needs proper maintenance and lubrication. The only thing needed is to disassemble the rifle enough for proper cleaning and lubrication. The receiver is three-sided stamped sheet metal. The rear trunnion and forward barrel trunnion are secured by rivets. Bolt rails are welded in place on the interior of the receiver. This receiver is rigid and strong. The barrel is a hard press fit tied in with a pin. The AK-47 is a model of reliability, but I have seen plenty of problematic rifles. Poor maintenance and haphazard manufacture lead to problems. When field stripping the rifle, first remove the magazine and then double check the chamber. Now look to the button at the rear of the receiver cover. Press this button to release the receiver cover. The forward receiver cover fits neatly into a semicircular slot in the rear sight assembly. If not properly fitted into this slot, the rear of the cover will not drop to allow the release button to click back into place. When the button is pressed in, the receiver comes out rear first. The bolt carrier is retained by the receiver and recoil spring guide. The bolt carrier rides on rails in the top of the receiver. It is well secured. The cover only keeps debris out of the rifle; it doesn't secure the action. To remove the

This is the AK bolt head, 5.56mm. Keep it clean!

recoil spring guide, press it forward and compress the recoil spring into the bolt carrier. The spring guide will come out of its slot in the rear trunnion. At this point, you will lift and pull up the recoil spring assembly from the bolt carrier. Next, grasp

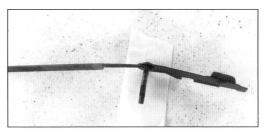

The author is performing a common field expedient. He is opening the safety on an AK variant for smoother function.

the bolt handle and pull the bolt to the rear by this handle. The bolt must travel completely to the rear and into the notches behind the slide rails of the AKM-type receiver. The bolt may then be lifted out of the receiver. The gas piston remains in the gas cylinder at this point, and you will not be able to lift the bolt carrier. However, you may lift the bolt carrier off the slide rails and lift it enough to get the bolt from the receiver. Then carefully pull the carrier to the rear and the gas piston will slip out of the gas cylinder. The bolt is rotated until the lug clears its raceway in the bolt carrier, and then the bolt is pressed forward and removed. A latch on the side of the receiver just under the rear sight allows the gas cylinder to be removed. The handguard and gas cylinder are removed in this manner. *The work begins now.* Scrub the bolt, gas cylinder, and gas piston, and pay close attention to the bolt face.

SUMMARY

The rifle is a precision instrument. When well maintained it may last a lifetime. A quality firearm is fascinating for its own sake, but—most importantly—the demands of personal defense, hunting, and target shooting as a sport are fully met by the rifles and equipment I have presented in this book. I hope you have enjoyed this work, and that the information discussed here will serve you well.